New Directions for Institutional Research

John F. Ryan
EDITOR-IN-CHIEF

Gloria Crisp
ASSOCIATE EDITOR

Partners in Advancing Student Learning: Degree Qualifications Profile and Tuning

Natasha A. Jankowski
David W. Marshall
EDITORS

Number 165
Jossey-Bass
San Francisco

PARTNERS IN ADVANCING STUDENT LEARNING: DEGREE QUALIFICATIONS
PROFILE AND TUNING
Natasha A. Jankowski, David W. Marshall (eds.)
New Directions for Institutional Research, no. 165
John F. Ryan, Editor-in-Chief
Gloria Crisp, Associate Editor

NEW DIRECTIONS FOR INSTITUTIONAL RESEARCH (ISSN 0271-0579, electronic
ISSN 1536-075X) is part of The Jossey-Bass Higher and Adult Education
Series and is published quarterly by Wiley Subscription Services, Inc.,
A Wiley Company, at Jossey-Bass, One Montgomery Street, Suite 1200,
San Francisco, California 94104-4594 (publication number USPS 098-
830). POSTMASTER: Send address changes to New Directions for Insti-
tutional Research, Jossey-Bass, One Montgomery Street, Suite 1200, San
Francisco, California 94104-4594.

INDIVIDUAL SUBSCRIPTION RATE (in USD): $89 per year US/Can/Mex,
$113 rest of world; institutional subscription rate: $341 US, $381
Can/Mex, $415 rest of world. Single copy rate: $29. Electronic only–
all regions: $89 individual, $341 institutional; Print & Electronic–US:
$98 individual, $410 institutional; Print & Electronic–Canada/Mexico:
$98 individual, $450 institutional; Print & Electronic–Rest of World:
$122 individual, $484 institutional.

EDITORIAL CORRESPONDENCE should be sent to John F. Ryan at
jfryan@uvm.edu.

New Directions for Institutional Research is indexed in Academic Search
(EBSCO), Academic Search Elite (EBSCO), Academic Search Premier
(EBSCO), CIJE: Current Index to Journals in Education (ERIC), Contents
Pages in Education (T&F), EBSCO Professional Development Collection
(EBSCO), Educational Research Abstracts Online (T&F), ERIC Database
(Education Resources Information Center), Higher Education Abstracts
(Claremont Graduate University), Multicultural Education Abstracts
(T&F), Sociology of Education Abstracts (T&F).

Cover design: Wiley
Cover Images: © Lava 4 images | Shutterstock

Microfilm copies of issues and chapters are available in 16mm and 35mm,
as well as microfi che in 105mm, through University Microfilms, Inc., 300
North Zeeb Road, Ann Arbor, Michigan 48106-1346.

www.josseybass.com

THE ASSOCIATION FOR INSTITUTIONAL RESEARCH (AIR) is the world's largest professional association for institutional researchers. The organization provides educational resources, best practices, and professional development opportunities for more than 4,000 members. Its primary purpose is to support members in the process of collecting, analyzing, and converting data into information that supports decision making in higher education.

CONTENTS

EDITORS' NOTES   1
Natasha A. Jankowski, David W. Marshall

1. Degree Qualifications Profile (DQP) and Tuning: What Are   3
They and Why Do They Matter?
Natasha A. Jankowski, David W. Marshall
In this introductory essay, Jankowski and Marshall offer a general
overview of both the Degree Qualifications Profile and Tuning and ex-
plicate elements of work with both that are of particular relevance to
offices of institutional research (IR). They also consider the potential
benefits institutions can garner by engaging with the DQP and Tuning.

2. The Role of Institutional Research in Institutional   15
Engagement with DQP and Tuning
Natasha A. Jankowski, Jillian Kinzie
Jankowski and Kinzie survey different ways in which IR has been involved with initiatives that undertake the DQP and Tuning to address
concerns with student learning and/or program effectiveness. The essay
focuses on different roles that IR might assume to participate in initiatives and includes some reflection on the types of roles that IR has yet
to take on.

3. Testing the DQP: What Was Learned About Learning   27
Outcomes?
Jessica L. Ickes, Daniel R. Flowers
The first of three case studies, this essay describes work by St. Mary's
College (Notre Dame, Indiana) to use the DQP as a point of comparison for learning outcomes in both general education and departmental
programs. Ickes and Flowers describe how the college's office of IR facilitated both this activity and a survey of student responses to the DQP's
outcomes and then reflect on the key lessons learned.

4. IR's Role in Piloting an Assessment Model: Coordination,   43
Consultation, and Compromise
Robert A. Sweatman
In this second case study, Sweatman describes the process in Illinois
College's master of education program to revisit an assessment pro-
gram in reference to the DQP. With attention to the project's particular
emphasis on rubrics, Sweatman explains how IR worked with faculty,
applied rubrics to measure student learning, and worked with results.

5. The DQP in Practice: A Framework of Dilemmas Facing   61
Institutional Researchers in Community Colleges
Sandra Fulton Bath
Fulton Bath reflects on work done at Reynolds College that used a
Tuning-type process with the DQP. The essay positions the DQP as
a consensus framework and differentiates it from a variety of other
frameworks before describing a "framework of dilemmas" (drawing on
Windschitl's work on constructivism) that challenged Reynolds' office
of IR as they worked with the DQP.

6. New Directions for IR, the DQP, and Tuning   77
Natasha A. Jankowski, David W. Marshall
In this concluding essay, Jankowski and Marshall describe the most re-
cent work being done with the DQP and Tuning, as well as similar ini-
tiatives in the United States en route to discussing the implications for
IR raised by the volume's case studies and these most recent examples.
The essay concludes that shifts in data use on campuses may require
shifts in how IR provides data and to whom.

INDEX   89

EDITORS' NOTES

In recent years, two tools have emerged as valuable resources for institutions and organizations interested in analyzing student learning outcomes, curricula, pedagogies, and outcomes assessment: the Tuning process, which was introduced to the United States in 2009, and the Degree Qualifications Profile, which followed 2 years later. Since then, over 600 institutions nationally have taken up the Tuning process or the Degree Qualifications Profile (DQP) to address institutionally or organizationally specific concerns about student learning. This volume of *New Directions for Institutional Research* aims to provide an introduction to the DQP and the Tuning process to those working in institutional research (IR). That introduction is intended to stimulate reflection and discussion on the role that offices of institutional research can play in projects involving work with each tool. The emphasis of this volume is on practical strategies by which IR can engage in collaborative work with the DQP and Tuning.

In the essays that follow, the contributors to this volume address several distinct aspects of recent work with the DQP and Tuning. The volume begins with an introduction to Tuning and the DQP, what they are, and what IR may need to know about them. The following essay by Natasha A. Jankowski and Jillian Kinzie outlines the various ways in which institutional research has been involved in DQP and Tuning efforts, bolstered by institutional examples, and outlines four roles for IR in the work. The essay by Jessica Ickes and Daniel Flowers provides a case example of IR involvement from the Higher Learning Commission (HLC) project. Their chapter focuses on the process of gathering and providing feedback to the first iteration of the DQP document, outlining some of the regularly received feedback from the pilot testing efforts, and offers lessons learned regarding implications for other IR offices. Following is another example from the HLC pilot by Robert Sweatman. A large majority of the DQP projects used rubrics in the assessment of student learning. Sweatman's chapter describes how an IR office oversaw the development and use of rubrics to assess student learning, providing useful references and considerations for others involved in rubric use. Sandra Fulton provides lessons learned from working with the Quality Collaboratives project under the direction of Association of American Colleges & Universities. Her chapter shares insights gained from engaging with DQP and Tuning as it relates to issues of transfer when a 2-year and a 4-year institution work in partnership. Pulling from various representational frameworks, she presents the various elements needed for consideration for those interested in beginning work with DQP and Tuning in terms of exploration of the shared understandings and possible dilemmas

NEW DIRECTIONS FOR INSTITUTIONAL RESEARCH, no. 165 © 2015 Wiley Periodicals, Inc.
Published online in Wiley Online Library (wileyonlinelibrary.com) • DOI: 10.1002/ir.20119

inherent in large-scale reflection and alignment exercises. The concluding essay provides a glimpse to the future and alerts IR professionals to related initiatives as well as provides an update to ongoing work with DQP and Tuning. Pulling from the prior chapters it provides some implications for IR offices to consider, not only in their work with the DQP and Tuning, but in terms of general decision support.

Natasha A. Jankowski
David W. Marshall
Editors

NATASHA A. JANKOWSKI, PHD, *is associate director of the National Institute for Learning Outcomes (NILOA) and research assistant professor with the Depart-ment of Education Policy, Organization and Leadership at the University of Illinois Urbana-Champaign.*

DAVID W. MARSHALL, PHD, *is associate professor of English at California State University San Bernardino and works with the Institute for Evidence-Based Change (IEBC) on Tuning work in the United States.*

NEW DIRECTIONS FOR INSTITUTIONAL RESEARCH • DOI: 10.1002/ir

1

This chapter provides a brief overview of the Degree Qualifications Profile and related Tuning process, summarizing lessons learned from institutional engagement with both. The value and purpose for working with each are explored.

Degree Qualifications Profile (DQP) and Tuning: What Are They and Why Do They Matter?

Natasha A. Jankowski, David W. Marshall

Institutional researchers may have noticed discussion of two related initiatives, each focused on enhancing clarity around student learning outcomes, which depart from the reporting concerns of access, persistence, and completion. These initiatives have involved over 600 institutions working with the Degree Qualifications Profile (DQP), a flexible profile of reference points of student learning, and its discipline-specific cousin, Tuning. Sponsored by Lumina Foundation, both projects are informed by other countries' efforts in this area (Adelman, 2009; Gaston, 2010). DQP is a learning-centered framework for what college graduates should know and be able to do upon completion of an associate's, bachelor's, or master's degree (Lumina Foundation, 2014). Tuning is a process by which faculty in a state, a region, or a discipline association from different institutions within a specific field determine learning outcomes for their subject area through consultations with one another, colleagues, students, alumni, and employers (Institute for Evidence-Based Change [IEBC], 2012).

The setting for the introduction of the DQP and Tuning to U.S. higher education comes at a moment when institutions are being asked to demonstrate whether the value of attending is worth the cost—basically addressing issues of the value added by a college education. Regional accreditors require institutions to define student learning outcomes and assess them, using the data to improve student learning. Policy makers want to ensure that institutions are being held accountable and students are graduating and gaining employment upon completion. Students want to make sure that what they are learning will help them get a job and advance their career. In response to these areas of concern and others, IR provides data—tons of data. There are reports on retention, graduation, cost, fact books, state accountability reports, Integrated Postsecondary Education Data System, and more. But one significant question has been talked about much less: when a student graduates with a degree, what does that degree represent? What are students actually getting and what is higher education validating when it confers a degree? Is it a certificate for time spent in a seat? Is it a reward for accumulation of Carnegie credit hours? Is it an acknowledgement for completion of a series of required courses? All of these suggest what a degree may represent in terms of numbers. But what do degrees represent in terms of learning? That is the question the DQP and Tuning try to address. The DQP provides reference points for what students should know and be able to do, regardless of major, in five areas of proficiency, at three successive degree levels. Tuning is a faculty-driven process of determining, within a specific field, what a student should know or be able to do upon completion of a degree (Lumina Foundation, 2014). Both the DQP and Tuning focus on moving the conversation away from proxy measures of student success to examination of student learning as the metric of interest.

This issue of *New Directions for Institutional Research* is designed to provide background and lessons learned, along with institutional examples, for institutional researchers interested in staying informed of these two initiatives or in engaging with them. In the following pages, we explain what the DQP and Tuning are and entail along with what we have learned in the tracking of DQP and facilitation of Tuning. This introductory chapter lays the groundwork of detailing the two initiatives, and the remaining chapters in the issue explore more fully the role of IR in DQP and Tuning efforts.

What Is Tuning?

Tuning is a procedural framework through which faculty define the essential student learning that constitutes a degree in a specific discipline (IEBC, 2012). The result is a set of learning outcomes, often scaled to degree level, that faculty in a department can use for aligning curricula and cocurricula, pedagogies, assignments, and expectations. In this way, the outcomes function as reference points for review and revision of curricula and praxis within specific programs and disciplines. Although this description may make Tuning seem like any other approach to outcomes development and use, what makes Tuning unique is the particular component processes that comprise the procedural framework overall. Participants in Tuning initiatives:

1. Define a discipline core (initial development of learning outcomes)
2. Map career pathways (identification of transferable skills and employment trajectories)
3. Consult stakeholders (communication and collaboration with interested parties)

4. Hone the discipline core (revision of learning outcomes)
5. Implement the core locally (use of learning outcomes in departments)

As may be apparent, Tuning offers something like an ethos for working on issues of student learning, insofar as its fundamental mode of work is faculty driven, stakeholder inclusive, and collaborative. Tuning encourages efforts to communicate not just within a faculty but across a campus (including students and alumni), multiple institutions, and sectors (such as civic offices or industry), so that the resulting learning outcomes are informed by and inform those stakeholders.

Tuning began in Europe in 2000 (Gonzalez & Wagenaar, 2003) and then came to Latin America in 2005 (Beneitone et al., 2007) before its arrival in the United States in 2009. Since work began in 2009, 21 disciplines have undergone a Tuning process with two disciplines tuning at a national level: history (sponsored by the American Historical Association) and communication (sponsored by the National Communication Association). The other 19 disciplines were addressed in state-based projects or, in the case of marketing and psychology, as part of a multistate regional project in Indiana, Illinois, and Missouri (sponsored by the Midwest Higher Education Compact). The remaining disciplines and the states that sponsored their Tuning projects are:

- Biology (Minnesota, Kentucky, Texas)
- Biomedical engineering (Texas)
- Business (Kentucky, Texas, Montana)
- Chemical engineering (Texas)
- Chemistry (Texas)
- Civil engineering (Texas)
- Electrical engineering (Texas)
- Elementary education (Indiana, Kentucky)
- Graphic design (Minnesota)
- History (Indiana, Utah)
- History education (Utah)
- Industrial engineering (Texas)
- Mathematics (Texas)
- Mechanical engineering (Texas)
- Nursing (Kentucky)
- Physics (Utah)
- Physics education (Utah)
- Social work (Kentucky)

Tuning's capacity to harmonize disciplinary degree expectations led to its initial use in 2009 to "tune" disciplines in these state-based projects in which representative faculty from universities across a state convened regularly to draft the discipline core outcomes that would then be used at each institution (Lumina Foundation, 2014). In this way, the expectations inherent in a degree in, say, history would have a common understanding among history departments around a state; students would work toward the same learning, though how particular programs in history achieve that learning (through specific curricula, pedagogies, or assignments) may differ according to each institution's particular approach. Such a process of statewide agreement has implications for transfer as well as curricular cohesion and transparency of program purpose to students.

One of Tuning's fundamental values is autonomy and valuing of institutional uniqueness. Because the learning outcomes collaboratively developed are used as reference points, individual institutions might increase the stated expectations or undertake radically different strategies for supporting students' attainment of them. They may revise or adapt them, align them to their own learning outcomes, or adopt them for their program. An institution's particular version of education in the discipline is often described in a Degree Specification. Degree Specifications are multifunctional documents that explain the purpose of a degree in a particular discipline, the defining characteristics of a particular program, the career skills and trajectories resulting from study in the discipline, the program's approach to teaching students, and the outcomes that students attain. The Degree Specification, in effect, serves as a profile of the program offered by a department that has worked through a process of responding to the discipline core outcomes developed in the Tuning project. In this way, the discipline core outcomes function for discipline-specific programs similarly to the way the DQP functions for an institution. For example, having recently completed the discipline core learning outcomes, participants in the National Communication Association's (NCA) project are entering the current academic year poised to engage their home faculty in processes of alignment, mapping, curriculum/pedagogy reviews and revisions, and development of assignments aligned to outcomes. The resulting shape of each program will be captured in a separate degree specification that, when set alongside all the others, will reveal the key differences that distinguish one department's program from others.

Whereas these larger scale projects strove to create comparability among different institutions and their programs in particular subject areas, institutionally specific DQP projects saw departments undertaking Tuning in ways that did not involve collaboration with other institutions. In these projects, Tuning offered a strategy for individual departments to work through their own engagement with the DQP by defining their own outcomes in relation to the DQP's proficiencies and through consultation with other programs and offices on their campuses.

Regardless of the scope of the project, Tuning offers an approach to consensus building and quality assurance that is driven by faculty efforts to define what quality means in terms of student learning (Jankowski & Marshall, 2014). The Tuning process fosters conversations among faculty, who are rarely trained as educators, around thinking pedagogically and devising more intentional educational programs that use outcomes-oriented strategies to student success in their disciplines. Such discussions benefit institutional effectiveness by giving faculty an increased stake in assessment by allowing them to define what "success" and therefore quality mean in the areas of their specialty. It also helps to redefine the role of faculty in assessment by allowing faculty to engage in assessment activities that are integrated into curricular activities. Ideally, Tuning is a recursive process, with faculty returning to outcomes and stakeholder input periodically, evaluating the degree to which the outcomes still suffice for the discipline.

What Is the Degree Qualifications Profile (DQP)?

The DQP is a profile of reference points regardless of a student's field of specialization that describes "in concrete terms how students demonstrate expected proficiencies across different degree levels and across the different elements of any degree" (Lumina Foundation, 2014, p. 6). It was written by four authors: Cliff Adelman, a senior associate at the Institute for Higher Education Policy; Peter Ewell, vice president of the National Center for Higher Education Management Systems; Paul Gaston, trustees professor at Kent State University; and Carol Geary Schneider, president of the Association of American Colleges and Universities (AAC&U is also the association responsible for the Liberal Education America's Promise (LEAP) Essential Learning Outcomes (ELOs)). The DQP is composed of five areas:

- Specialized knowledge, or what students should demonstrate with respect to their field of study
- Broad and integrative knowledge, where students apply and integrate learning from different broad fields
- Intellectual skills, composed of analytic inquiry, use of information resources, engaging diverse perspectives, ethical reasoning, quantitative fluency, and communicative fluency
- Applied and collaborative learning, emphasized by what students do with what they know
- Civic and global learning, where students engage with and respond to civic, social, environmental, and economic challenges

In part, DQP work began after Tuning was underway in the United States based on an assumption that once faculty engaged in a field-specific learning outcomes process, they would inevitably turn to generic outcomes associated with the degree level at issue, basically moving toward the need for a degree qualifications profile on their own. Other countries with centralized ministries call this a framework. They posit a few broad learning outcome statements that everyone adopts. In contrast, the U.S. version covers associate's, bachelor's, and master's degrees, regardless of field of specialization. Furthermore, the shape of the profile uses these as reference points, meaning institutions may choose to set the bar higher, they may adapt some proficiency statements and not include others, or they may adopt all of them and add others—that is why it is a profile and not a framework (Adelman, Ewell, Gaston, & Schneider, 2014). Thus it allows for experimenting and modification to the institution in question so that faculty can engage in an approach that is aligned to their work and allows for various elements of an institution's mission to come to the forefront. And although this provides an outline that the institution fills in and modifies accordingly, it is assumed that all learning outcome statements must be governed by active, operational verbs (Adelman, 2015) that logically lead to faculty-generated assignments that elicit student behaviors focused on integration and connection of learning experiences (Hutchings, Jankowski, & Ewell, 2014).

When the DQP was first introduced in 2011 in a beta form, various organizations were invited to undertake a testing of the document to see what might be done with it and, as multiple projects unfolded, one thing became clear quickly: there are multiple ways in which people understand and engage with the DQP, meaning there is not "a way" to do it (Jankowski & Marshall, 2014).

In the beta version, several projects were funded to foster experimentation with the DQP as well as to provide feedback to the four authors for the revision that was released in October 2014. Regional accreditor led projects included 29 institutions in the Western Association of Schools and Colleges (WASC) exploring various uses of the DQP, which subsequently led to the inclusion of the DQP in the June 2013 WASC guidelines as an option for institutions to ensure their degree is more than the sum of its individual parts. The Higher Learning Commission (HLC) asked a network of 23 colleges to explore the DQP through their Open Pathways and to share their feedback for the revision. Two of the chapters in this issue come from institutions working with the HLC project. The conversations that emerged from the work proved fruitful, in the words of one project participant, to "bring diverse campus groups together including faculty, students, contingent faculty and administration." The Southern Association of Colleges and Schools Commission on Colleges (SACSCOC) undertook a project with 22 historically Black colleges and universities, pairing one private and one public to examine curricula mapping in relation to the DQP proficiencies, and the Accrediting Commission for Community and Junior Colleges (ACCJC) engaged cohorts of institutions to explore better communication and transparency to external audiences around the meaning of the degree and issues of continuous improvement.

In addition to the projects led by regional accreditation agencies, several national membership organizations facilitated DQP related projects. The Council of Independent Colleges selected 25 institutions to explore the applicability of the DQP to independent, liberal-arts-oriented colleges. The

Association of American Colleges and Universities fostered Quality Collaboratives between 2-year and 4-year partner institutions and the American Association of State Colleges and Universities explored the use of the DQP at a system level.

Feedback from each of these projects as well as institutions that independently began working with the DQP was systematically collected and fed into a revision. Feedback from the field also led to the development of supporting materials for DQP implementation efforts, institutional examples, and a website (http://degreeprofile.org) where interested colleges and universities may go to learn more about this work. The revision of the DQP, driven by the feedback from the pilot projects and the field, led to clarification on some areas of note that are worth mentioning here:

1. Reiteration that the student, not the institution, is the primary point of reference within the DQP.
2. Focus on progressions of learning through articulating increasing levels of challenge.
3. Emphasizing the degree as opposed to the field of study.
4. Using active verbs to propose an integrated approach to student learning focused on what *all* students, as opposed to a sample, are able to demonstrate in regard to their learning across multiple teaching and learning experiences.

The DQP authors state that although accountability efforts rely largely on measures from standardized test scores, licensure exams, or student reports in surveys, the DQP "offers qualitative guidance both to students and to a society that asks, 'So you hold this degree. What does this mean you know and can do?'" (Lumina Foundation, 2014, p. 5). Yet it does so without relying on learning goals developed by individual institutions.

Commonalities Between DQP and Tuning

Regardless of whether an institution is working with the DQP or engaging in Tuning, both initiatives share commonalities including faculty being the heart of these efforts and driving the work alongside a continual focus on actual lived educational experience of students. In some ways, DQP and Tuning are about facilitating conversations to develop shared understandings on outcomes; yet, the shared understandings cannot be held by faculty alone. Although faculty drive the discussions of degree-level learning or discipline-based knowledge and skills, the integration of the agreed-upon learning outcomes across the educational enterprise requires collaboration and exploration of the entire campus community. These initiatives both touch upon the creation of coherent, intentional, sequenced, and integrated educational pathways that are clearly communicated to students throughout their time with the institution. To ensure that the agreed-upon outcomes are adequately addressed and assessed, both DQP and Tuning participants undertake a process of curriculum mapping. Identifying where learning occurs, how it scaffolds over time, and where there might be gaps or areas of departmental or institutional distinctiveness has helped institutions explore student experiences and quality assurance mechanisms internal to the institution as well as redesign curriculum to enhance efficiency and effectiveness. Moving from shared understanding of learning outcomes to indicating where learning occurs via curriculum mapping has also led to explorations of the role of course-embedded assignments (Ewell, 2013) along with issues of recordkeeping or alternative transcripts.

Although there are commonalities and institutions tend to undertake similar approaches to the work, as we have mentioned elsewhere there is no single best way to introduce and implement the DQP and/or Tuning (Jankowski & Marshall, 2014). Instead the process is local in nature and responsive to individual institutional context. Thus, although a collaborative process involving conversations and shared meaning-making with many other key members of the educational community including alumni and employers is undertaken, it is done so with a focus toward helping the institution meet its particular needs and goals. It is problem driven and institutionally specific. For both DQP and Tuning, therefore, respect for the particularities of a given institution are paramount. Each encourages internal reflection and is driven by the concerns specific to the institution undertaking work with them—in essence it is driven by the problems or questions identified by the institution or faculty (such as general education, transfer, alignment, etc.).

Because of the institutional specific nature of the work and the reflection on educational and curricular development, it is not surprising that what has been reported by participants in both Tuning and DQP work as having the most impact thus far are the conversations. Individually and together, Tuning and DQP provide the time and space to talk with colleagues and those in other disciplines about how best to foster and develop student learning along with how to create alignment in order to help students reach the proficiencies in question. The work has also brought a much needed student lens to bear, not just through a focus upon career pathways for students, but in terms of the realizations regarding how students navigate through an educational system to acquire requisite knowledge and skills. It has also involved bringing together various sources of data from across an institution in support of making decisions about the design and organization of educational opportunities and processes, unearthing assumptions and beliefs about students and how and where they learn. Working with DQP and Tuning thus requires creation of space for dialogue across the institution, invites a cognitive shift in thinking about higher education in terms of a collective and comprehensive view of learning, and works best when connected with existing initiatives or projects on campus. Norm Jones from Utah State University in a presentation at the 2014 Assessment Institute in

Indianapolis has gone so far as to argue that Tuning and DQP offer means for drawing together the disparate projects that have, on so many campuses, yielded initiative fatigue among faculty and staff alike.

Indeed, he may be right. Elsewhere (Jankowski & Marshall, 2014), we have identified the six shared goals and principles of DQP and Tuning work:

- *Creation of intentional pathways* for learning that build over time involves scaffolded credentials and coherent pathways for students across the entire institution.
- *Sequenced integrated learning experiences* are focused on the transfer of knowledge and skills scaffolding student learning experiences that are developmentally appropriate but also bring together various learning through application along with real world experiences.
- *Transparency and portability of learning* for students entails not only fostering metacognition and communicating clearly to students regarding their learning outcomes, but also detailing explicitly the implicit construction of the curriculum.
- *Quality assurance* of educational degrees and programs focuses upon the acquisition of evidence about what students know and can do with their learning by stressing that every student receives formative feedback through their educational experience to improve.
- *Inclusion and equity* involves actively implementing best practices to help advance student learning and student success while closing achievement gaps through guided pathways, curriculum coherence, transparency, and enhanced portability.
- *Collaboration* requires that we partner with those we may not have before to better understand how students actually experience our institutions and how we can best support students to move through them, among them and successfully out of them.

Many of these disparate projects share elements of the key goals undergirding the DQP and Tuning, potentially making these tools the effective means Jones described of pulling different projects together.

What Do We Know About DQP and Tuning Work?

Since 2001, the National Institute for Learning Outcomes Assessment (NILOA) has been involved in tracking work with DQP and Tuning through various means to better understand how institutions are undertaking the work as well as to determine its possible impact on students and their learning. This volume incorporates information pulled from various data collection processes undertaken by NILOA including web crawlers and web scans, institutional self-reports, observations of Lumina-funded project work, and institutional surveys of participating institutions. Of the over 600 institutions working with DQP and Tuning, the majority have been public, but private and for-profit institutions have engaged as well. Institutions have used the DQP at various levels including program and institution level, and general education, with some engaging in cocurricular conversations and connecting with employers. Institutions use DQP proficiency statements and Tuning documents for clarification and review of outcomes, curriculum mapping and revision, general education reform, transfer and articulation, program development and review, accreditation reports, strategic planning, and assessment of student learning. Possibilities for different ways to engage with the outcome statements are high in part because original pilot projects were intentionally asked to find different ways to use the DQP and identify the many educational problems that it might be helpful to address.

Institutions have continued to use DQP and Tuning to refine and revitalize the core curriculum, strengthen academic program review, develop new programs, revise the first-year seminar, integrate academic affairs with cocurricular learning, improve academic advising, enhance transfer, and reinvigorate assessment. This work has helped institutions think more systematically about educational experiences as well as view learning from the student perspective. One faculty participant stated that the DQP and Tuning have compelled faculty to "think collectively about the course sequence and program as well as degree in ways we never had before." DQP and Tuning projects have been highly touted for fostering space for conversations and reflection on if the educational offerings institutions have developed and provided are working in the ways that institutions thought they were. DQP and Tuning conversations have led faculty and administrators to unearth assumptions about how and where students learn, how they are or are not communicating learning opportunities and outcomes to students and whether the institution is being intentional, coherent, and integrative in learning experiences for all students.

Summary

In summary, the DQP offers a degree qualifications profile, exclusive of discipline in five interrelated as opposed to discrete proficiencies. In essence it is a product that implies a process. It is also undertaken as an institutional process across disciplines and may involve partner institutions in terms of transfer. Tuning on the other hand is about disciplinary qualification profiles, and it describes a process that gets to a product of the learning outcomes for a specific discipline and degree. Tuning work occurs across multiple institutions, at a state level, regional level, or disciplinary association level.

Neither the DQP nor Tuning specify what should be taught or outline how to deliver content. Neither do the DQP and Tuning limit learning to that which occurs in courses. This work involves understanding that the completion of courses or accumulation of hours is not a meaningful proxy for learning. And this work requires demonstration, by all students, that they have achieved the faculty-determined levels of proficiencies. The DQP provides a common language for talking about what students should know and be able to do along with reference points focused on student learning as opposed to job placement rates or test scores of graduates (Jankowski, Hutchings, Ewell, Kinzie, & Kuh, 2013).

References

Adelman, C. (2009). *The Bologna process for U.S. eyes: Re-learning higher education in the age of convergence.* Washington, DC: Institute for Higher Education Policy. Retrieved from http://files.eric.ed.gov/fulltext/ED504904.pdf.

Adelman, C. (2015, February). *To imagine a verb: The language and syntax of learning outcomes statements.* (Occasional Paper No. 24). Urbana, IL: University of Illinois and Indiana University, National Institute for Learning Outcomes Assessment.

Adelman, C., Ewell, P. T., Gaston, P. L., & Schneider, C. G. (2014). The Degree Qualifications Profile 2.0: Defining US degrees through demonstration and documentation of college learning. *Liberal Education, 100*(2), 32–35.

Beneitone, P. et al. (2007). *Reflexiones y perspecivas de la Education Superior en America Latina. Informe Final—Proyecto Tuning—America Latina 2004–2007.* Bilbao, Spain: Universidad de Deusto.

Ewell, P. T. (2013, January). *The Lumina Degree Qualifications Profile (DQP): Implications for assessment* (Occasional Paper No. 16). Urbana, IL: University of Illinois and Indiana University, National Institute for Learning Outcomes Assessment.

Gaston, P. L. (2010). *The challenge of Bologna.* Sterling, VA: Stylus Publishing.

Gonzalez, J., & Wagenaar, R. (2003). *Tuning educational structures in Europe. Informe final—Proyecto Piloto, Fase 1.* Bilbao, Spain: Universidad de Deusto.

Hutchings, P., Jankowski, N. A., & Ewell, P. (2014, November). *Catalyzing assignment design activity on your campus: Lessons from NILOA's assignment library initiative.* Urbana, IL: National Institute for Learning Outcomes Assessment and Institute for Evidence-Based Change.

Institute for Evidence-Based Change. (2012). *Tuning American higher education: The process.* Encinitas, CA: Author.

Jankowski, N. A., Hutchings, P., Ewell, P., Kinzie, J., & Kuh, D. (2013). The Degree Qualifications Profile: What it is and why we need it now. *Change: The Magazine of Higher Learning, 45*(6), 6–15.

Jankowski, N. A., & Marshall, D. W. (2014). *Roadmap to enhanced student learning: Implementing the DQP and Tuning.* Urbana, IL: National Institute for Learning Outcomes Assessment and Institute for Evidence-Based Change.

Lumina Foundation for Education. (2014). *The Degree Qualifications Profile.* Indianapolis, IN: Author.

NATASHA A. JANKOWSKI *is associate director of the National Institute for Learning Outcomes Assessment and research assistant professor in the department of Education Policy, Organization and Leadership at the University of Illinois Urbana-Champaign.*

DAVID W. MARSHALL *is associate professor of English at California State University San Bernardino and serves as director of Tuning USA with the Institute for Evidence-Based Change.*

NEW DIRECTIONS FOR INSTITUTIONAL RESEARCH • DOI: 10.1002/ir

2

This chapter discusses the role of institutional research in DQP and Tuning work. Examples from the field of the myriad ways in which IR has been involved, as well as an exploration of ways in which IR has yet to be involved, are discussed.

The Role of Institutional Research in Institutional Engagement with DQP and Tuning

Natasha A. Jankowski, Jillian Kinzie

This chapter frames the essays that follow by broadly surveying the various roles taken by institutional research (IR), working closely in collaboration with offices of assessment, in Degree Qualifications Profile (DQP) and Tuning initiatives. Supported by examples from the field, possible roles of IR are presented to demonstrate different ways in which IR has engaged with, coordinated, or led DQP and Tuning efforts.

The Varied Roles of Institutional Research

The role of institutional research is varied and vast. In regard to DQP and Tuning efforts, the most salient connection between IR and work with the DQP and Tuning is through efforts related to assessment and decision-support. This linkage is supported by IR's expanding role in institutional effectiveness and its connection with assessment of student learning (Bers, 2008). Frederick Volkwein (2011) argues that "student learning outcomes are central to the purpose of educational organizations, and the assessment of these outcomes supplies some of the most important evidence demonstrating institutional effectiveness" (p. 3). He goes on to state that IR's role is broader than that of compiling fact books or accountability reports because, "IR now serves as a major vehicle for gathering and delivering evidence of educational effectiveness" (p. 3). More specifically, findings from a 2008 survey of IR task hierarchies indicate that IR offices were involved in evaluation and assessment related tasks including student outcomes research (64%), assessment of general education (62%), and evaluations of student services (60%) (Volkwein, 2011)—all areas in which DQP and Tuning projects have focused. Institutional researchers' support of various

NEW DIRECTIONS FOR INSTITUTIONAL RESEARCH, no. 165 © 2015 Wiley Periodicals, Inc.
Published online in Wiley Online Library (wileyonlinelibrary.com) • DOI: 10.1002/ir.20121

15

assessment efforts was further demonstrated in a survey of provosts regarding learning outcomes assessment practices wherein provosts reported that offices of IR supported organizational assessment efforts "quite a bit" (Kuh, Jankowski, Ikenberry, & Kinzie, 2014). Thus, although not directly leading the efforts, IR has been involved with and at the table for various institutional conversations to provide support for decisions, showcase available data, and coordinate institution-wide efforts around understanding student learning (Bers, 2008). Regardless of whether assessment is housed in institutional research or in its own office, whether they work in concert or separately, IR and assessment offices both serve a function of providing data and evidence for fostering institutional improvement and external reporting.

Yet, the roles of IR have not always been focused on institutional effectiveness, decision support, or broader collaborations across college and university units. In fact, the roles of IR have shifted over time and continue to do so. In 1993, Patrick Terenzini outlined three areas in which IR professionals are involved under the heading of organizational intelligence, a term mentioned in relation to IR by Fincher (1978), involving technical and analytical intelligence, issues intelligence, and contextual intelligence. Technical and analytical intelligence focus upon the reporting function of IR whereas issues intelligence has more to do with being aware of the data needs of decision makers and proactively meeting those needs. Contextual intelligence brings an understanding of the placement of the institution in a wider, external environment and the potential for changing data needs due to environmental shifts. This perspective on IR's significant organizational intelligence role makes IR a gateway for various offices and personnel within the institution regarding available data that may be used to enhance decision making. However, this positioning of IR is not without detractors. IR offices have been viewed as data hoarders by some within the institutional community, or too busy with external reporting to participate in campus initiatives, let alone lead campus initiatives. As the chapters in this issue demonstrate, IR offices are well positioned to lead the type of work undertaken in relation to defining degree-level learning outcomes. The movement in the field toward collaboration and cooperation to inform decision making signals a larger shift in the role of IR offices to one that is actively involved across colleges and universities.

Beyond reporting functions and support for decision making (Saupe, 1990), IR offices have been involved in engaging in a social process of knowledge construction (Woodley, 1999), fostering buy-in to systematic processes (Reynolds-Sundet & Adam, 2014), and/or helping to create a culture of inquiry (Brittingham, O'Brien, & Alig, 2008). Further, IR has been involved with curriculum development or instructional design (Wehlburg, 2006), program design (Delaney, 2009), and strategic planning efforts (Voorhees, 2008). IR practitioners have been described as problem-solving knowledge workers (Calderon & Mathies, 2013), information architects (Matier & Sidle, 1995), and expert witnesses (Fincher, 1997). These roles

NEW DIRECTIONS FOR INSTITUTIONAL RESEARCH • DOI: 10.1002/ir

require knowledge of organizational behavior (Schmidtlein, 1999) in addition to understanding faculty work (Middaugh, Kelly, & Walters, 2008), and they also require an awareness of the entire institutional community and their respective data needs in addition to ongoing projects or initiatives. This expanded level of awareness of current institutional initiatives and data needs is relevant to DQP and Tuning projects.

To meet these different roles, IR professionals may use a "consultancy-like" skill set involving knowledge of how other units operate, their data needs, and moving between and among different areas of campus (Calderon & Mathies, 2013). Volkwein (1999) describes the Janus-like nature of the IR professionals who must navigate between internal and external, academic and administrative cultures, and institutional and professional roles. Bers (2008) states "because IR is not part of a specific academic department, it brings a neutral perspective to the assessment conversation" (p. 34). In addition, it serves as a central repository for a variety of longitudinal data and is able to pull from various data sources across campus—a skill set useful for DQP projects that aim to better understand how students experience the entirety of the collegiate experience.

In 2015, the Association for Institutional Research (AIR) initiated a project to examine shifts in IR roles. From the brief summary of the pilot "Statements of Aspirational Practice for Institutional Research" the authors argue for a widening of the lens of decision support and what constitutes decision makers. The statement offers a vision of IR as collaborative partners working with the entire campus community to "share, collect, interpret, and use data" (p. 1). Further, the statement highlights the shift from an institution-level lens to a student-focused enterprise by asking how various elements support and enhance student experiences, arguing that the means to support such work is through coordination of various efforts and partnering across offices and units—foci that are apparent in other literature on IR roles mentioned prior and a needed skill set in IR involvement in DQP and Tuning efforts.

Over time the IR office continues to shift from providing accurate indicators and numbers or statistics and data points, toward facilitating meaning-making of data and providing support in analysis and evaluation efforts. The shifting nature of the role of IR to one of decision support for various decision makers and partner or coordinator of data efforts, uniquely positions IR staff to be a vital part of DQP and Tuning efforts in colleges and universities. We turn now to examples of the ways in which IR have been involved in DQP and/or Tuning work.

Institutional Examples

Six brief examples help illustrate the varying roles of IR in institutional efforts to engage with the DQP and Tuning. The examples shared here are drawn from the National Institute for Learning Outcomes Assessment

NEW DIRECTIONS FOR INSTITUTIONAL RESEARCH • DOI: 10.1002/ir

(NILOA) Institutional Activity Reports used to collect information on DQP and Tuning efforts; they are offered as brief entry points to possible IR involvement in the work and to help frame the four roles this chapter outlines for IR in the subsequent section. The following three chapters in this issue provide a more comprehensive discussion of IR processes and involvement from the perspective of those directly undertaking the work.

IR as Leader.   St. Olaf College in Minnesota involved IR in concert with the faculty-led assessment committee when they first reviewed the DQP in relation to the articulation of their institution-wide learning outcomes. The Office of Institutional Research and Evaluation led the discussions to ensure that an across the college lens was emphasized in conversations. Further, given the scope of the institution-wide examination of learning outcomes in cocurricular contexts (including student employment) as well as in curricular contexts with feedback gathered from across the campus community including students, IR offered significant input into specifying outcomes and identifying possible sources of evidence. IR synthesized community feedback on the institutional learning outcomes, and the office now uses the revised goals as a framework to organize and report available data, allowing for identification of and filling of gaps in evidence. Further, organizing reports around the outcomes allowed IR to be part of multiple cross-campus conversations where academic programs and various offices that provide support to one or more of the outcomes could come together to make sense of the data and determine ways to improve student learning.

IR as Partner.   Lane Community College in Oregon involved their IR office from the inception of working with the DQP as a member of a larger project team. The director of the Office of Institutional Research, Assessment and Planning was part of a cross-campus team, serving as chair of the college assessment team. The DQP was explored in relation to Lane's Core Learning Outcomes to align institution-wide learning outcomes with a national framework and to map student learning to the aligned outcomes. Other members of the institutional team included deans, faculty (full and part time), student affairs staff, librarians, assessment directors (including the general education assessment coordinator), instructional designers, and information technology specialists who helped design mapping tools. The director of IR was involved in the conceptualization of the work, actively participated in project meetings, and provided insight into available data on various aspects of the project. Work with the DQP informed Lane's descriptions and definitions of their Core Learning Outcomes and has led to the development of a beta-version of a mapping tool which allows faculty to connect course outcomes to Core Learning Outcomes and include sample assignments that provide evidence of student learning assessment and proficiencies.

IR as Data Support.   The accounting program at Concordia University in Wisconsin began working with the DQP through an examination

NEW DIRECTIONS FOR INSTITUTIONAL RESEARCH • DOI: 10.1002/ir

of the learning outcome category of Specialized Knowledge at the baccalaureate level. Although their project initially focused on the development of measurable learning outcomes for two milestones in the accounting program—the end of the first year when students were able to formally enter the degree program and at the point of degree completion in their fourth year—the work quickly turned to conversations of connections to general education. Faculty within the accounting program mapped their degree curriculum as well as the business core courses within the college and general education requirements. Through this mapping process and subsequent discussion, the faculty determined they needed to measure student performance at the completion of the first year of the program as well as at the fourth year, but not solely for the accounting program. They also needed to examine student learning within the business core courses and general education, thus amassing a collection of evidence looking across all the outcomes students were to address. This focus led to an exploration of the four other learning outcome categories of the DQP beyond Specialized Knowledge and required the accounting faculty to work across departmental and school boundaries, including partnering with IR. The director of institutional research became involved when the project moved beyond a focus on the accounting department to examining the success of accounting majors from the courses where year one and year four assessments took place. Further, IR was involved in integration with the learning management system and responding to faculty questions about whether students who transferred into the major at different points in time were as successful as native students in the business core courses, general education, and the accounting program itself. Finally, it was determined that additional assessment measures were needed to understand the progression of student learning, and IR was involved in the conversations around the development of such measurements.

IR as Faculty Support.   Faculty from Fullerton College in California participated in a Tuning project and subsequently brought the discipline core document back to the department for review. Within the department, faculty met and agreed on a set of student learning outcomes for their program, informed by the Tuning developed document, and set about to assess student learning in relation to the outcomes. Through conversations, they decided to assess student learning in voluntary internship experiences for students and used the reports IR provides to departments to craft program review self-studies to better understand student experiences. In addition, they created course-embedded assignments and classroom-based performance assessments, engaging in interdepartmental dialogue about curriculum, course pairing, and degree requirements; embedding of Tuning concepts into lesson plans and syllabi; and connections with off-campus groups such as a community organizations, high school parents and faculty, local employers, and families. In addition, the faculty worked with local 4-year institutions on issues of transfer, which involves transfer data on students as well as course-taking patterns. The work with Tuning provided a means for faculty to actively engage with assessment, but also to communicate the value of the program to the public and administrators, supported in part by data provided by IR.

IR as Evidence Support.   Faculty within Avila University in Missouri examined the Tuning documents developed in a larger statewide conversation to improve undergraduate psychology curriculum by changing the structure and sequence of courses as well as mapping learning outcomes and assessment to specific courses. Faculty who participated in the discussions, mapping, and curricular revision developed a much clearer conception of the outcomes they expect students to achieve and were able to articulate to potential and current students how and why they were striving to meet those outcomes and future career goals. The modified curriculum is believed to better prepare students, based on data provided from partnering with IR. For instance, many of the students in the spring capstone course (which occurred post curricular changes) were offered employment at their practice sites, something that had never happened before. In addition, IR was involved in areas of transfer as the department worked to ensure the 200 course-level classes were transfer friendly and has led to conversations on how to revise the general education core, supported by IR involvement.

IR and Transfer.   Salt Lake Community College faculty aligned their departmental learning outcomes with the Tuning statements developed by the American Historical Association and also helped to "tune" the departments across the state of Utah to the document. They began exploring issues of transfer around levels of student learning, examining what a student in a 2-year program needs to know and be able to do to succeed in the third and fourth year of their major. The transfer conversation was undertaken in partnership with IR because, as one faculty participant stated, "it made us more mindful that we do not and must not work in a vacuum, and that to truly provide students the education they need, we must work in concert with the institutions to which they transfer." In addition, they provided training to adjunct faculty on the learning outcomes as well as the rationale for the outcomes. Specifically, IR has been involved in tracking the success of students at the end of their first year at the transfer institution and upon completion of the 4-year degree. IR is also involved in comparisons of student performance to that of nontransfer students.

Role of IR in DQP/Tuning Efforts

Given the wide scope and evolving nature of IR functions it is not surprising that IR has been involved in a variety of ways across DQP and Tuning projects. In fact, the role of IR in DQP and Tuning projects has been as varied as the projects themselves. As mentioned in Chapter 1, institutions working with the DQP have done so for various reasons including mapping to a national profile, examining and revising learning outcomes statements, facilitating 2- to 4-year transfer, and assessing student learning. For example, faculty participants in Tuning engaged in surveying employers and other stakeholders in relation to the drafted learning outcomes, and upon returning to campus, began using discipline core documents in various ways related to issues of retention, communication to incoming students and employers, and program review and improvement. Thus in some manner the involvement and role of IR depends in part on the type of project and work being done. However, from the NILOA tracking of institutional work with DQP and Tuning, lessons learned across projects lend themselves to inform the role of IR in this work.

The first lesson from our review of institutional work with the DQP and Tuning is that IR must be involved from the onset. DQP projects in particular need IR directly engaged from the inception of the work. Whereas some of the DQP projects begin in an academic department focused on mapping their curriculum and aligning their outcomes with the DQP, the conversations quickly move outside of the department in terms of exploring the role of general education in the major, or equivalent institutional core curriculum. At this point, IR may become involved for purposes such as disaggregating data by majors or exploring students' course-taking patterns. However, without involvement from the start of the project, the purpose for such data requests may be unclear and the ability for IR to proactively engage in the data needs of faculty participants might be limited. For Tuning, IR needs to be informed when faculty within their institution are participating in Tuning conversations with other faculty outside of the institution in order to be prepared to assist faculty participants in surveying relevant stakeholders as part of the Tuning process. Further, if IR is aware when faculty are participating in external Tuning conversations, they can better position themselves to provide support to faculty upon returning to campus by examining students within the discipline in light of the shared Tuning core document.

Second, although not all IR offices have assessment-related responsibilities, the expertise of IR in thinking through issues of data collection and outcomes assessment is vital to DQP and Tuning work. Faculty-led mapping of student learning outcomes and curriculum in relation to the DQP and/or Tuning discipline core routinely ends up in conversations involving rubrics and assignment design (Hutchings, Jankowski, & Ewell, 2014). Moving the focus of assessment to course-embedded assignments aligned with outcomes at the program, general education, or institution level requires IR's thoughtful participation in exploration of alignment, data capture, and consistency of collection across programs and levels. Being involved from the beginning of projects, sharing awareness of various sources of evidence already available across a college or university, and participating in the conversations related to assignment design and embedded assessment position IR to better understand data needs as well as the technological requirements or systems needed to "roll-up" reporting from the various levels.

Additional insights about the role of IR emanated from sessions conducted at the 2015 AIR Forum in Denver. In these sessions we shared examples of institutional work with the DQP and Tuning and how IR has been involved, and then engaged in discussion about IR specific concerns and questions. Although IR participants were familiar with the DQP, they were less familiar with Tuning and were eager to hear more about what institutions were doing in their projects and how that work might affect their offices. Encouragingly, IR professionals expressed that as part of their professional responsibility it is important to stay abreast of trends, developments, and movements in the field of higher education and to be informed of the DQP and Tuning work occurring nationally. Further, their conversations and concerns focused upon the need for assessment support, consistency in data collection, and shared understanding of learning outcomes to better determine evidence that would be sufficient to address issues of quality assurance. They discussed how to report information in meaningful ways to engage with various audiences internal and external to the institution and how to support this work on their own campuses as it related to ongoing initiatives and efforts.

Overall, IR professionals are critical to involve in DQP and Tuning efforts. However, additional clarity about possible roles and the identification of anticipated data reporting and assessment needs would provide greater support for their meaningful participation. Pulling from the prior examples and to illustrate the range of IRs involvement in DQP and Tuning we provide four possible roles for IR in this work.

Four Roles for IR

In looking across the various examples shared in this chapter as well as the exploration of the roles of IR broadly within the field, we make an argument for four ways in which IR can be involved in DQP and Tuning work. We offer these as a starting point or foundation, but reiterate that the role of IR will shift focus depending on the nature of the work itself.

Getting to the Table.   First, IR needs to be a part of the conversation from the beginning, helping to alert participants to existing data, looking across the various sources of evidence available, and helping project teams to avoid re-collecting existing data or oversurveying students. In looking across the examples shared in this chapter, even those that started in one department spread to an institution-wide lens, required more nuanced understanding of students and their movement through educational experiences via disaggregation. In addition, IR can be on the front end of helping participants think about survey design or other evidentiary needs, such as the example of surveying students outlined in the chapter in this issue by Jessica Ickes and Daniel Flowers.

NEW DIRECTIONS FOR INSTITUTIONAL RESEARCH • DOI: 10.1002/ir

Collaborating and Coordinating.   Second, when working on a DQP and/or Tuning project, IR will need to actively seek out connections, working with various segments of campus that may be undertaking different strands of work in order to ensure that data collection processes, training, fidelity of implementation, and validation of collected data occur in a systemic way. The chapter in this issue by Robert Sweatman provides an example of how IR might facilitate and coordinate across campus DQP or Tuning efforts. This role is also in alignment with the current AIR discussions around IR practice in terms of collaborating broadly across colleges and universities, and helping to ensure that data collection, as well as meaning-making efforts related to decision making, are coordinated and involve active participation from multiple campus constituents while adhering to issues of data quality.

Facilitating Alignment.   Third, IR has a role in facilitating alignment across educational levels as DQP and Tuning shift the focus from an institution-level lens to a student-focused one. Part of that shift has involved mapping outcomes to assignments and using assignments embedded in courses as a means of "rolling up" to provide evidence for an institution-level view of student learning. IR can provide support in thinking through the implications of this approach for data collection, validation, and analysis. Robert Sweatman's chapter provides an example of considering alignment, as does Sandi Fulton's chapter exploring transfer issues. Even if an institution is not involved in DQP or Tuning work, this role proves salient because provosts indicated that the most useful information on student learning is that of course-embedded assignments (Kuh et al., 2014). Although the difficulty of aggregating up results to an institution-level has been an obstacle to institutions moving toward course-embedded assessment (Volkwein, 2011), some progress can be seen in the NILOA occasional paper on the work of Prince George Community College (Richman & Ariovich, 2013) as well as that undertaken in the Multi-State Collaborative (see Crosson & Orcutt, 2014).

Organizing Data for Decision Making.   Finally, in sharing evidence and providing data or reports to inform decision making, IR should consider crafting reports around agreed upon outcomes to continue to foster shared meaning-making and to provide a means to bring multiple sources of evidence together in support of better understanding students and their learning. This is especially important since the majority of DQP and Tuning work involves a formative view of processes and learning as opposed to a summative one, such that as students are moving through an institution, data are fed back to inform changes in order to help current students continue to advance to achieve the agreed upon learning outcomes. This role is in alignment with questions which IR are suited to answer including where the student, program, or institution is meeting educational goals and whether the student or program is actually improving (Volkwein, 2011).

Final Thoughts

As institutions of higher education endeavor to enhance the learning experience for all students and ensure they are equipped with the knowledge, skills, and abilities needed for success, more attention will be afforded to reference points outlined in learning-centered frameworks like the DQP and processes for determining discipline-specific learning outcomes as in Tuning. Both initiatives provide strategies for addressing contemporary campus issues related to general education, transfer articulation and success, accreditation, and most important, the assessment and improvement of student learning. This work to articulate and demonstrate what every graduate at a given level ought to know and be able to do and focus on the processes and experiences to achieve these outcomes, demands the involvement and skills of institutional research. Institutional research must be an active partner in and coordinator of data across institution-wide and department-level efforts to experiment with and relate DQP and Tuning to institutional goals.

Notably, several elements of DQP and Tuning have transformational potential for higher education and likewise for the broad duties and functions of IR. One of the transformational aspects of the DQP is the shift from current degree-progress markers of number of courses or credit hours completed, and the awarding of degrees from measures of accumulated number of credits and grade point averages, to a qualitative set of learning outcomes that describe what degrees mean in terms of demonstrated student performance. This shift is understandably disruptive to a range of current campus data collection and reporting activities. Yet, IR can more likely facilitate consideration of approaches to recording student performance and progress and the data needed to inform decision-making if they are involved from the onset of DQP and Tuning projects and employ consultancy-like skills to understand and respond to various data needs.

Another transformational aspect of DQP and Tuning is the emphasis that both projects place on articulating learning outcomes within and across fields, degree programs, between the curriculum and co-curriculum, and among institutions. As the institutional examples illustrate, DQP and Tuning projects quickly move out of a department discussion of, for example, a history department curriculum, into general education and the cocurriculum, and even from 2- to 4-year institution. Given the need for a wide vantage point, and IR's data skills, IR can be well-positioned to serve or lead projects. However, this may require new roles for IR in coaching and assisting in institutional projects at all levels of the institution and beyond, as well as in the need to build the data literacy skills of faculty, student affairs and others outside of the traditional IR office.

We are describing a shift in the role of IR offices that puts them more toward the center of projects as campus facilitators and collaborators. The shifting nature of IR roles toward a more campuswide function of institutional research is consistent with the skills demanded by work with the

DQP and Tuning. As a vital partner in efforts to assure higher education's effectiveness and document student learning, IR must be involved in initiatives like DQP and Tuning that promise to help transform higher education.

References

Association of Institutional Research. (2015). *A brief summary of statements of aspirational practice for institutional research.* Retrieved from https://www.airweb.org /Resources/ImprovingAndTransformingPostsecondaryEducation/Documents/AIR%2 0Statements%20of%20Aspirational%20Practice%20for%20IR%20-%20Summary.pdf.

Bers, T. H. (2008). The role of institutional assessment in assessment student learning outcomes. In D. G. Terkla (Ed.), *New Directions for Higher Education:, No. 141. Institutional research: More than just data* (pp. 31–39). San Francisco, CA: Jossey-Bass. doi: 10.1002/he.291

Brittingham, B., O'Brien, P. M., & Alig, J. L. (2008). Accreditation and institutional research: The traditional role and new dimensions. In D. G. Terkla (Ed.), *New Directions for Higher Education: No. 141. Institutional research: More than just data* (pp. 69–76). San Francisco, CA: Jossey-Bass. doi: 10.1002/he.294

Calderon, A., & Mathies, C. (2013). Institutional research in the future: Challenges within higher education and the need for excellence in professional practice. In A. Calderon & K. L. Webber (Eds.), *New Directions for Institutional Research: No. 157. Global issues in institutional research* (pp. 77–90). San Francisco, CA: Jossey-Bass. doi: 10.1002/ir.20040

Crosson, P., & Orcutt, B. (2014). A Massachusetts and multi-state approach to statewide assessment of student learning. *Change: The Magazine of Higher Learning, 46*(3), 24–33.

Delaney, A. M. (2009). Institutional researcher's expanding roles: Policy, planning, program evaluation, assessment, and new research methodologies. In C. Leimer (Ed.), *New Directions for Institutional Research: No. 143. Imagining the future of institutional research* (pp. 29–41). San Francisco, CA: Jossey-Bass. doi: 10.1002/ir.303

Fincher, C. (1978). Institutional research as organizational intelligence. *Research in Higher Education, 8*(2), 189–192. doi: 10.1007/BF00992119

Fincher, C. L. (1997). Researchers as consultants and expert witnesses. In L. G. Jones (Ed.), *New Directions for Institutional Research: No. 96. Preventing lawsuits: The role of institutional research* (pp. 51–59). San Francisco, CA: Jossey-Bass. doi: 10.1002/ir.9606

Hutchings, P., Jankowski, N. A., & Ewell, P. T. (2014). *Catalyzing assignment design activity on your campus: Lessons from NILOA's assignment library initiative.* Urbana, IL: University of Illinois and Indiana University, National Institute for Learning Outcomes Assessment.

Kuh, G. D., Jankowski, N., Ikenberry, S. O., & Kinzie, J. (2014). *Knowing what students know and can do: The current state of student learning outcomes assessment in US colleges and universities.* Urbana, IL: University of Illinois and Indiana University, National Institute for Learning Outcomes Assessment.

Matier, M. W., & Sidle, C. C. (1995). Institutional researchers' roles in the twenty-first century. In T. R. Sanford (Ed.), *New Directions for Institutional Research: No. 85. Preparing for the information needs of the twenty-first century* (pp. 75–85). San Francisco, CA: Jossey-Bass. doi: 10.1002/ir.37019958509

Middaugh, M. F., Kelly, H. A., & Walters, A. M. (2008). The role of institutional research in understanding and describing faculty work. In D. G. Terkla (Ed.), *New Directions for Higher Education: No. 141. Institutional research: More than just data* (pp. 41–56). San Francisco, CA: Jossey-Bass. doi: 10.1002/he.292

Reynolds-Sundet, R., & Adam, A. J. (2014). Community college strategies. *Assessment Update, 26*(1), 12–14. doi: 10.1002/au.20003

Richman, W. A., & Ariovich, L. (2013). *All-in-one: Combining grading, course, program, and general education outcomes assessment.* (Occasional Paper No. 19). Urbana, IL: University of Illinois and Indiana University, National Institute for Learning Outcomes Assessment.

Saupe, J. L. (1990). *The functions of institutional research* (2nd ed.). Tallahassee, FL: Association for Institutional Research.

Schmidtlein, F. A. (1999). Emerging perspectives on organizational behavior: Implications for institutional researchers. In J. F. Volkwein & S. LaNasa (Eds.), *New Directions for Institutional Research: No. 104. What is institutional research all about? A critical and comprehensive assessment of the profession* (pp. 61–72). San Francisco, CA: Jossey-Bass. doi: 10.1002/ir.10406

Terenzini, P. T. (1993). On the nature of institutional research and the knowledge and skills it requires. *Research in Higher Education, 34,* 1–10. doi: 10.1007/BF00991859

Volkwein, J. F. (1999). The four faces of institutional research. In J. F. Volkwein & S. LaNasa (Eds.), *New Directions for Institutional Research: No. 104. What is institutional research all about? A critical and comprehensive assessment of the profession* (pp. 9–19). San Francisco, CA: Jossey-Bass. doi: 10.1002/ir.10401

Volkwein, F. J. (2011). *Gaining ground: The role of institutional research in assessing student outcomes and demonstrating institutional effectiveness* (Occasional Paper No. 11). Urbana, IL: University of Illinois and Indiana University, National Institute for Learning Outcomes Assessment.

Voorhees, R. A. (2008). Institutional research's role in strategic planning. In D. G. Terkla (Ed.), *New Directions for Higher Education: No. 141. Institutional research: More than just data* (pp. 77–85). San Francisco, CA: Jossey-Bass. doi: 10.1002/he.295

Wehlburg, C. (2006). *Meaningful course revision: Enhancing academic engagement using student learning data.* San Francisco, CA: Jossey-Bass.

Woodley, A. (1999). Doing institutional research: The role of the partisan guerrilla. *Open Learning, 14*(2), 52–58. doi: 10.1080/0268051990140207

NATASHA A. JANKOWSKI *is associate director of the National Institute for Learning Outcomes Assessment (NILOA) and research assistant professor in the department of Education Policy, Organization and Leadership at the University of Illinois Urbana-Champaign.*

JILLIAN KINZIE *is associate director of the Center for Postsecondary Research and NSSE Institute at Indiana University, as well as a senior scholar with the National Institute for Learning Outcomes Assessment (NILOA).*

3

Through a campuswide project using the Degree Qualifications Profile (DQP) as a comparison tool that engaged students and faculty, the authors share findings and implications about learning outcomes for IR professionals and DQP authors while considering the role of IR in large-scale, campuswide projects.

Testing the DQP: What Was Learned About Learning Outcomes?

Jessica L. Ickes, Daniel R. Flowers

Saint Mary's College (Notre Dame, IN) was given the opportunity to engage with the Degree Qualifications Profile (DQP) as part of a larger project through the Higher Learning Commission (HLC) to provide feedback to the framework's authors. An institutional project team led this work, coordinated by the college's Office of Institutional Research and Assessment. This case study shares key findings that emerged through the college's work with the DQP and discusses how that work influenced the institution's understanding of learning outcomes. In addition, this case study focuses on how institutional research (IR) affected this work and implications for IR that have emerged related to the DQP.

In 2011 Saint Mary's College, a small, private, women's Catholic liberal arts college in northern Indiana, was invited by its regional accreditor, the Higher Learning Commission, to pilot test its new model for accreditation. The HLC's revised model for accreditation is composed of two key processes, the assurance process and the improvement process (Higher Learning Commission, 2015). Whereas the assurance process focuses on assuring compliance with the core accreditation standards, the quality initiative of the improvement process encourages institutions to focus on internal institutional projects of significance or to work collaboratively on an improvement project with other institutions (Rogers, Holloway, & Priddy, 2014).

A cohort of colleges in the HLC region were invited to serve as "pioneers" of the new accreditation model, a pilot group that provided feedback to the commission regarding the revised assessment process. As part of the pioneer cohort of institutions, the group was asked to test the Degree Qualifications Profile as a collaborative improvement project. This pilot project

New Directions for Institutional Research, no. 165 © 2015 Wiley Periodicals, Inc.
Published online in Wiley Online Library (wileyonlinelibrary.com) • DOI: 10.1002/ir.20122

was funded by a grant from the Lumina Foundation to the Higher Learning Commission. The commission's charge to the cohort of institutions was broad, inviting each institution to develop projects to test the Degree Qualifications Profile and provide feedback to the commission that would be aggregated and given to the DQP authors prior to the revision of the beta version of the DQP framework (Rogers et al., 2014). At the same time, a number of other projects were occurring nationally through various organizations including the Council of Independent Colleges (CIC), the Association of American Colleges and Universities (AAC&U), and the Western Association of Schools and Colleges (WASC) (Lumina Foundation, 2014). The reports from each of these groups aimed to provide feedback to the authors on the beta version of the DQP that could be used in subsequent revision.

This was a particularly opportune time for the college to participate in this project. Saint Mary's had spent 4 years as a participant in the HLC Assessment Academy, investing resources to develop a campus culture of assessment that had the necessary competence and infrastructure to support robust assessment. The college's Office of Institutional Research and Assessment had collaborated with the faculty to successfully complete the HLC Assessment Academy and had developed significant knowledge of the accreditation process. During this time, the college was also undertaking a significant revision to its general education curriculum, moving from a distribution model of requirements to a curriculum based on learning outcomes, the Sophia Program (St. Mary's College, n.d.), which focused on learning across the 4 years of a student's education. The confluence of these works primed the campus to work with the DQP framework through a number of developed projects.

Project 1: General Education and Departmental Curricular Gap Analysis

A project team consisting of the provost, director of institutional research and assessment, assistant director of institutional research, and an assistant professor of biology developed two projects, each with two subprojects to thoroughly test the DQP framework. The first project intended to look broadly at the DQP and the Sophia Program, comparing the articulated learning outcomes of the DQP framework and the college's curriculum to identify areas of learning that were included in one curriculum but not in the other. We intended our comparison of the DQP outcomes to the learning outcomes at a unique institution like Saint Mary's to provide the DQP authors with feedback on curricular gaps as well as to give the college an early opportunity to review its own revised curriculum for any areas that may be in need of further refinement. Specifically, the team postulated that if a central aim of the DQP is to capture learning at the degree level, this

New Directions for Institutional Research • DOI: 10.1002/ir

project would help to identify any additional learning outcomes the DQP may want to address.

Methodology.   To accomplish this work, the project team formed seven groups of four to eight faculty and staff members to focus on individual DQP outcome groups. Faculty members and administrators were invited to participate based on their expertise in the area of the DQP to be examined. The Office of Institutional Research and Assessment played a critical role in identifying the appropriate colleagues to participate in these groups because of its familiarity with those in departments and divisions on campus. The IR office developed a common set of questions for each groups to address. These groups met to compare the DQP outcome group to the outcomes articulated in the Sophia Program. Members of these groups were also asked to identify the overall strengths of the DQP, as well as areas for improvement. This work produced a comparative gap analysis document for each DQP outcome group.

.   The Office of Institutional Research director and assistant director facilitated this work by both coordinating and moderating many of the group work sessions. This encouraged each group to thoroughly address the common questions, stay on task, and ensure a single voice did not dominate the conversation. The IR office then analyzed data from these groups in a methodologically responsible manner with qualitative grounded theory to identify common themes. To encourage broad campus engagement and diversity of opinion with this work, the gap analysis documents were presented for comment to faculty at an all-day faculty meeting and were shared with staff and administrators in open meetings after which the documents were made available to faculty, staff, and administrators using a wiki for final comment. More than two-thirds of full-time faculty members at the college participated in this project.

Comments from the various campus audiences were compiled by the Office of Institutional Research and were synthesized by DQP outcome groups. This initial synthesis produced a substantial (and somewhat unmanageable) volume of material, so the office further refined the synthesis to focus on significant gaps. This part of the project was enhanced by the partnership with IR due to the office's familiarity with summarizing large quantities of qualitative comments.

At the same time, a similar effort was underway to conduct a gap analysis within major programs of study specifically focusing on the DQP's Specialized Knowledge outcomes. Because the DQP asserts that the Specialized Knowledge outcomes apply to all academic programs of study within a degree, the gap analysis project was conducted in four self-selected academic programs. Academic departments were invited to participate and four diverse programs volunteered: nursing, modern languages, biology, and psychology. Similar to the overall collegewide gap analysis, each participating academic department created a comparative analysis document and included comments on the overall strengths and weaknesses of the DQP

NEW DIRECTIONS FOR INSTITUTIONAL RESEARCH • DOI: 10.1002/ir

Table 3.1. Nonviable Learning Outcome Gaps Between DQP and the Sophia Program

DQP Category	DQP Outcome Language
Communication Fluency	In a language other than English, and either orally or in writing, conducts an inquiry with a non-English-language source concerning information, conditions, technologies, and/or practices in his or her major field. (Lumina Foundation, 2011)
Applied Learning	Completes a substantial field-based project related to his or her major course of study; seeks and employs insights from others in implementing the project; evaluates a significant challenge or question faced in the project in relation to core concepts, methods, or assumptions in his or her major field; and describes the effects of learning outside the classroom on his or her research or practical skills. (Lumina Foundation, 2011)

framework. The Office of Institutional Research supported the academic departments as they carried out their work by preparing a comparative analysis document and synthesizing the findings across academic programs.

Findings.   There were few significant gaps between the DQP bachelor's level outcomes and the Saint Mary's College Sophia Program. The committee charged with the assessment of the Sophia Program, the Sophia Program Oversight Committee, reviewed the gaps identified between the DQP learning outcomes and the college's learning outcomes. The committee determined that the majority of gaps identified were intentional and based on specific curricular design. Where gaps were present, the committee noted that the Sophia Program outcomes often expected student learning at a more advanced level and required the student to demonstrate higher level thinking skills than did the DQP outcomes.

Two DQP learning outcome gaps were identified that were determined not to be viable at Saint Mary's College (Table 3.1).

Members of the campus community noted that the Communication Fluency gap would require foreign language ability at a higher level than is currently required of students in the Sophia curriculum and raised questions about who on campus would be capable of assessing the student achievement of the outcome (that is, finding faculty who are fluent in any second language in which a student would want to achieve this outcome and who could also assess appropriate content knowledge of the selected discipline). Faculty members also questioned whether it would be possible for all majors, spanning from the humanities to the professional majors, to complete a substantial field-based project particularly in disciplines that less often use this pedagogy. Additionally, faculty questioned whether there was appropriate infrastructure on campus and availability of opportunities in the field to require all majors to complete a substantial field-based project related to the major.

NEW DIRECTIONS FOR INSTITUTIONAL RESEARCH • DOI: 10.1002/ir

Table 3.2. Learning Outcome Gaps Considered by Sophia Program Committee

DQP Category	DQP Outcome Language
Analytical Inquiry	Differentiates and evaluates theories and approaches to complex standard and nonstandard problems within his or her major field and at least one other academic field. (Lumina Foundation, 2011)
Applied Learning	Completes a substantial field-based project related to his or her major course of study; seeks and employs insights from others in implementing the project; evaluates a significant challenge or question faced in the project in relation to core concepts, methods, or assumptions in his or her major field; and describes the effects of learning outside the classroom on his or her research or practical skills. (Lumina Foundation, 2011)
Information Resources	Explicates the ideal characteristics of current information resources for the execution of projects, papers, or performances; accesses those resources with appropriate delimiting terms and syntax; and describes the strategies by which he/she identified and searched for those resources. (Lumina Foundation, 2011)
Information Resources	Incorporates multiple information resources presented in different media and/or different languages, in projects, papers, or performances, with citations in forms appropriate to those resources, and evaluates the reliability and comparative worth of competing information resources. (Lumina Foundation, 2011)

A few gaps were identified by the Sophia Oversight Committee (Table 3.2) as warranting further consideration for potential changes to the Sophia Program.

The four DQP outcomes listed in Table 3.2 included the time period when analytical inquiry and applied learning outcomes would be achieved by students (in the major field of study or before). This specificity of time was not present in the Sophia Program outcomes. The information resources outcomes were noted to require a deeper level of cognition than is required in the Sophia Program because they require students to be able to describe strategies in the identification of resources. Some reviewers indicated that they thought the DQP language describing the area of learning as Use of Information Resources would be more easily understood by students than the Sophia's language of Information Literacy used to describe its outcomes. The oversight committee found this to be notable and indicated an interest in considering a potential change in the terminology. It was also noted that the Sophia Program does not require "multiple information resources be presented in different media and/or languages" (Lumina Foundation, 2011, p. 13) as is required in the DQP outcomes. Commenters expressed significant concerns that this outcome could be achieved by all bachelor's degree students. The most common concern focused on the suggestion that students could present multiple information resources in different languages. The faculty noted that the Sophia Program curriculum was not designed to develop foreign language skills in all students to the extent needed to achieve this outcome, nor would a small campus faculty have the skill set to assess the student achievement of the language component of this outcome.

Another key finding from the campuswide project focused on the extent to which outcomes may vary by degree level. The comparison project not only analyzed gaps at the baccalaureate level but also did so for the associate's and master's level even though the institution did not offer those degrees at the time. The analysis found that although the college only offered bachelor's degrees, the Sophia Program's outcomes were meeting or exceeding some of the master's degree-level outcomes. It was unclear to commenters what the implications would be of students meeting higher level outcomes than the degree program in which they were enrolled. For example, if the DQP outcomes at a degree level articulate the minimum achievement at that degree level, is there an upper bound within a degree level? Specifically, if a student enrolled in a bachelor's degree program achieves the master's degree level outcomes does this suggest they should also receive a master's degree?

Perhaps the chief benefit Saint Mary's College experienced as part of this project was the engagement of the campus community in a substantive discussion of both the DQP student learning outcomes as well as its own outcomes. The context of the DQP as a national framework helped focus the discussion on how a Saint Mary's education compares to a national framework. This project facilitated an intellectual engagement with learning outcomes that was welcomed by the campus community and allowed the campus to engage in critical analysis in a manner that was not threatening. This project helped to affirm the strengths of the college's curriculum as well as identify a few potential key modifications.

Additionally, in completing the comparisons of Specialized Knowledge outcomes conducted by academic departments, each department was able to align their major outcomes to the DQP outcomes at the bachelor's degree level. Departments also were invited to comment on the DQP outcomes. Concerns included unclear outcome language, implied curricular requirements, or when DQP outcomes were overly prescriptive in identifying media in which outcomes were to be achieved. For example, the following DQP Specialized Knowledge outcome was noted as lacking clarity:

- Generates substantially error-free products, reconstructions, data, etc. or juried exhibits or performances as appropriate to the field. (Lumina Foundation, 2011)

One department questioned, "What does error-free product mean exactly?" Related to outcome syntax, one academic department identified the following outcome as speaking more to an assessment measure rather than actual student learning:

NEW DIRECTIONS FOR INSTITUTIONAL RESEARCH • DOI: 10.1002/ir

- Constructs a summative project, paper, performance, or practice-based performance that draws on current research, scholarship, and/or techniques in the field. (Lumina Foundation, 2011)

Departments also identified a number of important major-level skills missing from the DQP Specialized Knowledge outcomes including collaborative skills, communication skills, integration, intercultural engagement, or the requirements of specialized or professional accreditation. Although the departments acknowledged that these "intellectual skills" appear elsewhere in the DQP document, it was suggested by multiple departments that learning these skills in the context of the academic major are of great importance for majors. For example, communication skills and intercultural engagement in the context of nursing is different than for students studying French or psychology but for each department their approaches to these skills are considered specialized disciplinary knowledge. Additionally, departments identified strengths of the DQP including the perceived use of a developmental hierarchy of learning by degree level and the attempt to enhance transparency and communicate what departments intend for students to learn in programs of study.

In addition to the institutional and departmental gap analysis, the Office of Institutional Research advised that the broad campus may have additional input for the DQP authors bringing in voices outside of those who participated in the gap analysis. The IR office facilitated and collected general comments to share with the DQP authors gathered from faculty and staff presentations and from a wiki that was made available to all institutional employees. The majority of the commenters focused on general comments regarding the language of the DQP outcomes. Employees frequently noted that the DQP outcomes were "overly prescriptive," specifically regarding how the outcome should be achieved or demonstrated (that is, in a paper, project, etc.) Interestingly, although the outcomes were often described as too specific, other comments suggested that the outcomes were too broad to be meaningful. Those providing feedback suggested that in some cases the outcomes were trying to accomplish too much within a single statement and suggested that this may be a consequence or challenge of trying to establish outcomes that fit the variety of institution types in U.S. higher education. Some reported that developing a national framework of outcomes could lead to or encourage a "lowest common denominator" effect where student achievement would be reduced to this threshold. Comments received from faculty illustrate this sense:

- "Potential to standardize curricula based on lowest common denominator. Could stifle independent pursuit of an area of excellence."
- "Here is the temptation to establish a minimum baseline and ignore higher level."

New Directions for Institutional Research • DOI: 10.1002/ir

A significant finding emerged as the project leaders worked through the synthesis of the information gathered through this project. As a Catholic women's college in the liberal arts tradition, Saint Mary's was attuned to how its mission might fit within a national framework of outcomes. The DQP tried to specifically address institutional/mission-related outcomes through an institution-specific outcomes category that would allow institutions to contribute its own unique learning outcomes. At the early stages in the project, there was a general appreciation for the DQP offering this category. However, as comments were analyzed and thinking developed, there was a strong sense that the DQP structure minimizes the central role of mission by relegating Institution Specific outcomes to a category "off to the side" of the other outcomes instead of attempting to understand how mission is integrated throughout learning outcomes as it informs, integrates with, and contributes to the entirety of student learning.

Project 2: Student Feedback on DQP Outcomes

The second project that Saint Mary's developed as part of the HLC DQP testing was the quality initiative project focused on providing students with the opportunity to give feedback on the achievement of the DQP outcomes in their major and to share their understanding of each DQP Specialized Knowledge outcome in the context of the major.

Methodology. The Office of Institutional Research and Assessment developed a survey instrument that was vetted by participating departments aimed at measuring (a) the extent to which students believed their major emphasized the DQP Specialized Knowledge outcomes and (b) the extent they believed their department contributed to their achievement of the Specialized Knowledge outcomes. A question that emerged at the onset of the project was whether students have similar understandings of the outcome language regardless of major, because the DQP Specialized Knowledge outcomes have the difficult task of being broad enough to apply to all academic disciplines. It was hoped that this survey would allow the college to incorporate the student perspective on the DQP outcomes into the feedback provided to the authors.

At most campuses, IR has a significant role in designing and administrating surveys. The office frequently has access to the tools and methods used to most effectively and efficiently administer such instruments. This ability was particularly helpful for this portion of the institutional project. IR designed an instrument that could address the questions raised by the project team both quantitatively and qualitatively. Surveys were administered electronically to junior- and senior-level majors in each of the four participating academic departments at the end of the academic year. The survey response rate was 50%. The Office of Institutional Research designed, administered, analyzed, and provided summaries of the results to the participating departments for consideration.

NEW DIRECTIONS FOR INSTITUTIONAL RESEARCH • DOI: 10.1002/ir

Findings.   Generally, students, regardless of academic major, indicated that their departments both emphasized and contributed to their achievement of all Specialized Knowledge outcomes in the DQP irrespective of the degree level of the outcome (Ickes & Flowers, 2013). Modern language majors indicated a slightly lower level of emphasis and contribution than did the biology, nursing and psychology majors. The project team speculated that this difference could be related to the relevance of these outcomes to the modern language major, as well as differing interpretation of the outcomes' phrasing, which may have affected student response. This difference raised questions about the universal applicability of the outcomes across programs of study in higher education (Ickes & Flowers, 2013).

Perhaps the most interesting findings of our DQP project emerged from the qualitative portion of the student survey. Students were asked to articulate in their own words what each bachelor's-level DQP Specialized Knowledge outcome meant in relation to their major. The survey presented each outcome to students and asked: "Please explain in your own words what the following learning outcome means and how it relates to your major" (Lumina Foundation, 2011). This question provided a unique opportunity for students to directly interpret the Specialized Knowledge outcome language in the context of their program of study.

Generally, students' interpretation of the outcomes suggest that they were able to understand the core concept of the outcome. Interestingly, though, when students approached the outcomes using their disciplinary perspective, there was variability noted in the way they interpreted key words and phrases. In many cases, this variation in interpretation was extensive enough that the meaning of the outcome was noticeably different (Ickes & Flowers, 2013). For example, in the DQP outcome "Defining and explaining the boundaries and major sub-fields, styles, and/or practices in your field" (Lumina Foundation, 2011), the word "boundaries" was interpreted in a variety of ways based on the student's academic discipline (Table 3.3). Nursing majors sometimes commented on the term "boundaries" as referencing professional boundaries in care provided (that is what a nurse is able to do compared to a doctor) whereas some modern languages majors interpreted the term "boundaries" as relating to global boundaries sometimes brought on by divides in language.

The variety in understandings of this one term frequently led students to interpret the outcome differently depending on their program of study. Similar examples were seen among other Specialized Knowledge outcomes.

As discussed previously, particular terms (in this case "fluency", Table 3.4) have a specific meaning within the context of the academic discipline. This can affect how students interact and understand the learning outcomes, which is a concern not only for the applicability of the outcomes to all academic programs but for IR and assessment professionals who seek to measure the achievement of student learning. If this variation in outcome interpretation affects what students actually aim to or do learn, it introduces

New Directions for Institutional Research • DOI: 10.1002/ir

Table 3.3. Student Interpretation of Select DQP Learning Outcomes—Boundaries

Outcome	Student Interpretation
Defining and explaining the boundaries and major subfields, styles, and/or practices in your field. (Lumina Foundation, 2011)	"Learning how and when to apply my knowledge of Spanish. To know about the dialects and history of the language so that it may be applied internationally rather than having knowledge just of one specific region of the world. The importance of the Spanish language in literature, art, and history. Knowing all the ways in which I can use my Spanish skills." "I think that understanding the boundaries in nursing applies to what is allowed within nursing practice, such as what a nurse cannot do whereas a physician can. The major subfields are explored within the different classes that are required in the major like oncology, OB, pediatric, etc. The styles and practices seem to indicate the interventions and understanding of practices of a nurse." "The word boundaries is a little confusing about exactly what is meant by it."

Table 3.4. Student Interpretation of Select DQP Learning Outcomes—Fluency

Outcome	Student Interpretation
Demonstrating fluency in the use of tools, technologies, and methods common to your field. (Lumina Foundation, 2011)	"I believe this learning outcome refers to the techniques and tools used to conduct biological experiments and collect and analyze data properly in a lab." "I can't really think of how the Spanish language uses tools and technologies." "Being able to communicate with a native speaker— includes understanding them as well as them being able to understand you."

an inconsistency that may not be adequately accounted for in measurements or in the analysis of assessment findings conducted by institutions and IR offices.

Key Findings: What Was Learned About Learning Outcomes?

1. National frameworks of learning outcomes such as the DQP can foster valuable conversations on campus about student learning and can serve as a comparison for examining institutional general education learning outcomes.
2. Students often understand the core meaning of specific learning outcomes but disciplinary perspectives may skew the interpretation if a shared understanding is not intentionally facilitated.

NEW DIRECTIONS FOR INSTITUTIONAL RESEARCH • DOI: 10.1002/ir

3. Special consideration should be given to how institutional mission influences and is threaded within learning outcomes.
4. Learning outcomes within the DQP were sometimes considered to be overly prescriptive and, at the same time, many faculty thought the wording was too broad to be meaningful.

These findings should be taken within the context of the limitations of this case study. These findings represent only one, small, relatively homogeneous institution. In large part due to the size of the institution, the number of participants, both students and faculty, was small. Likewise, findings related to the Specialized Knowledge outcomes were tested among only four academic programs.

Implications

The findings from the studies point to two sets of implications, one for IR practitioners and another for DQP authors to inform the 2014 revision of the DQP. Implications for each are presented as they relate to the projects undertaken at Saint Mary's.

For IR Practitioners.   As the college undertook and completed this series of projects, we learned that IR offices are uniquely positioned within institutions to facilitate engagement on campus around institution-wide projects such as the DQP. Although other offices on campus may be capable of leading and facilitating this kind of project, IR has the technical knowledge to also guide the development of research around a large-scale project and the knowledge of research design and analysis to help an institution make informed use of the results from such a study. We found that the confluence of these skills allowed our IR office to function both in a leadership role and analytical role, synthesizing data, in this type of a project. Although IR offices are not always sought for this type of leadership role, our experience with this project suggests it may be a valuable and untapped resource for colleges working on these types of initiatives or projects.

One of the key benefits of the Office of Institutional Research playing a leadership role in campuswide projects is based on a fundamental role of IR in building relationships across campus and developing broad institutional knowledge. IR offices frequently collaborate with many faculty members and administrative offices to gather needed data and to encourage data-driven decision making on campus (Howard, McLaughlin, & Knight, 2012). In this role, IR can encourage a variety of people with different perspectives and skill sets on campus to engage with campuswide projects like the DQP. Administration is often hesitant to ask faculty to participate in this type of project because of already existing demands on their time. In this case study and its series of projects, institutional research found that faculty and academic departments were pleased to participate in this type of project provided that the administrative tasks associated with it were handled by administration. In this way, IR was able to play a key role in project management, data collection, analysis, and synthesis in order to allow faculty to engage with the ideas of the DQP and the task of providing thoughtful feedback to the project. This was helpful both in facilitating the administration of the project in a timely manner and in maintaining faculty engagement without bogging them down in the administrative components of the project. Additionally, institutional research was able to suggest the potential benefit of including the student perspective in the project adding a critical and unique view to the analysis. The office was able to logistically facilitate the student involvement in collaboration with the academic departments in a way that encouraged high rates of participation.

As in this case, IR was also able to help translate key findings from the DQP projects into actionable items for a campus to consider. For example, the finding in this case study that suggests student variation in the interpretation of learning outcomes led the IR office at Saint Mary's College to suggest studying how students interpret and understand the college's learning outcomes. This has led the college to consider whether to implement a model of advising as a form of teaching on campus to serve as a key point of engagement with students in order to help them understand the meaning and expectations of the college's learning outcomes. In another example, the discussions around the DQP outcomes facilitated by IR generated praise and critique for the DQP authors, while giving project participants a chance to think critically about learning outcomes. We hope this served as a professional development activity as we heard similar discussion subsequently emerge around the wording of the college's own outcomes. Essentially the project process facilitated by institutional research was able to serve as a replicable template for other conversations about outcomes on campus.

The work of IR on national or institution-wide projects like the DQP can serve as small pilot or case studies to encourage more thorough research in the field. One of the key findings of this project aligns to the research around the Tuning project and suggests that learning outcomes may not be interpreted consistently. Because the assessment literature also notes the importance of clearly written student learning outcomes that communicate expectations between faculty and students (Suskie, 2009), these findings suggest an opportunity both nationally and institutionally for IR offices and other researchers to study this in greater depth and compare alternative strategies to improve "norming" around learning outcomes.

IR professionals are often well-versed in higher education policy and initiatives typically developed through the study of higher education trends and an attention to the higher education landscape to provide context to the work they do. This makes IR a valuable team member in working on an institution-wide project and keeping institutions informed of the national context and emerging next steps in the project. Although institutional priorities often shift, the broad view of IR can keep the institution abreast of national projects and particularly the DQP over a long term.

NEW DIRECTIONS FOR INSTITUTIONAL RESEARCH • DOI: 10.1002/ir

Although IR offices may be well positioned to take on these types of projects, it can be a hindrance as it competes with time for other IR projects. In the case of this project, the IR work was coordinated primarily by two IR administrators with periodic support from the provost's administrative assistant. Because the DQP project was incorporated in our accreditation work, it was given institutional priority. Participation in large-scale projects of this type may be hampered due to other IR or institutional priorities as well as limitations on staffing particularly at small institutions.

The authors of this chapter suspect that the impact of the DQP framework and its companion project around Tuning will continue to affect IR in a variety of ways in upcoming years. As time allows, we would encourage IR professionals to follow the path of the DQP as it expands in its usage and to engage when possible in discussions around the use of this type of framework. The influence of the DQP framework thus far has been broad and has begun to be used as a framework for or foundational document for discussion around initiatives such as a certificate and credential registry, an expanded transcript model, and the Carnegie Classification revision in 2018 (Degree Qualifications Profile, n.d.). These additional initiatives may have relevance to IR offices, such as how proficiencies are recorded on campus, and in any impact it may have on the Carnegie Classification revision, which has implications for rankings, grants, and comparative groups.

For the Revised DQP.   Since the conclusion of the Higher Learning Commission testing of the Degree Qualifications Profile, the DQP was revised by its authors based on beta testing from "more than 400 colleges and universities in 45 states (Lumina Foundation, 2014). The authors used the feedback generated through these interactions with institutions to revise the document and address concerns that were raised. The authors have clarified the purpose of the DQP and have indicated that the document aims to "define quality," serve as an accountability measure, and that the "proficiencies are intended not as statements of aspiration for some students, but as descriptions of what every graduate at a given level ought to know and be able to do" (Lumina Foundation, 2014, p., 4). In the revision, the authors of the DQP also added a key section to the document explaining how to interpret the DQP learning outcomes or proficiencies. This section responds to comments noting the prescriptiveness of outcomes, suggesting that assignments, etc. should only be interpreted as examples for reference and that the minimum proficiencies do not preclude a higher level of proficiencies being required by an institution's curriculum and the depth of instruction in particular areas. (Lumina Foundation, 2014). The revised DQP document acknowledges a number of uses of the DQP (Lumina Foundation, 2014), most often as a framework, but the authors of this case study note that many of the examples in the revised document could infer an adoption of the DQP by institutions and accreditors.

In our testing projects, those working on the projects found that the idea of a national framework of learning outcomes by degree level made

New Directions for Institutional Research • DOI: 10.1002/ir

intuitive sense. The idea that a degree means that students have achieved certain learning outcomes did not seem radical to those involved with this project (Ickes & Flowers, 2013). Additionally, faculty and administration at Saint Mary's found the document to be a useful tool with which to compare an institution's general education curriculum to a national framework in order to identify curricular gaps and by which to encourage lively academic debate about the merits of making curricular modifications to address these gaps.

Other key findings from this case study pose broader philosophical questions for the DQP, its use as a framework, or potential adoption. Faculty as well as administrators working closely with the framework on these projects were concerned regarding the level of prescriptiveness of the learning outcomes. In the revised DQP document, there has been revision to language to minimize this and to clarify the purpose of the document and the outcomes themselves to note a lack of intention to be prescriptive.

Finally, the results from this project suggest that the DQP reconsider how they account for institution-specific outcomes within the framework in a subsequent revision. Each regional accrediting body requires institutions to evidence how their mission is integrated throughout the institution as well as how well it is achieved. Mission does not exist in a vacuum. The relegation of these outcomes to "add-on" outcomes, to the side of the framework, seems to be contrary to the good practice that would encourage mission to influence and evidence itself through outcomes throughout the curriculum.

Conclusion

What we learned about learning outcomes throughout these projects was used along with feedback from other national and institutional projects to revise the Degree Qualifications Profile in addition to illustrating ways in which IR offices can contribute to institution-wide and national projects of significance. At an institutional level, the inclusion of student perspectives in our work provided insight on how we approach assessment and learning outcome language. At the pivot point of these interactions, well-functioning and supported campus IR Offices are often poised not only to provide technical expertise to such projects but also to serve as coordinators, bridging the gap between campus and national initiatives and facilitating work that can have lasting impacts on individual campuses as well as on broader policy.

References

Degree Qualifications Profile. (n.d.). *Related initiatives.* Retrieved from http://degreepro file.org/related-initiatives/.

Higher Learning Commission. (n.d.). *The Open Pathway: HLC pathways for reaffirmation of accreditation*. (n.d). Retrieved from https://www.ncahlc.org/Pathways/open-pathway.html.

Howard, R. D., McLaughlin, G. W., & Knight, W. E. (Eds.). (2012). *The handbook of institutional research*. San Francisco, CA: Jossey-Bass.

Ickes, J., & Flowers, D. (2013). Student interpretation of selected degree qualifications profile outcomes. *Assessment Update, 25*(4), 1–2, 14–16. doi: 10.1002/au.254

Lumina Foundation for Education. (2011). *The Degree Qualifications Profile*. Indianapolis, IN: Author.

Lumina Foundation for Education. (2014). *The Degree Qualifications Profile* (2nd ed.). Indianapolis, IN: Author.

Rogers, G., Holloway, A., & Priddy, L. (2014, April). *Exploring degree qualifications*. Chicago, IL: Higher Learning Commission. Retrieved from http://www.learningoutcomeassessment.org/documents/HLCFinalReport.pdf.

St. Mary's College. (n.d.). *Sophia Program in Liberal Learning: Saint Mary's College 3.0*. Retrieved from https://www.saintmarys.edu/files/CG3.pdf.

Suskie, L. (2009). *Assessing student learning: A common sense guide* (2nd ed.). San Francisco, CA: Jossey-Bass.

Jessica L. Ickes is the director of institutional research at Lebanon Valley College in Annville, PA and former director of institutional research and assessment at Saint Mary's College in Notre Dame, IN.

Daniel R. Flowers is the director of institutional research and former assistant director of institutional research at Saint Mary's College in Notre Dame, IN.

This chapter focuses on IR's role in coordinating a pilot of the Degree Qualifications Profile (DQP) for assessment in a new master's degree program and provides guidance on frameworks that can be used, important technical considerations, and ways IR can be involved to advance the use of rubrics as a primary program assessment tool.

IR's Role in Piloting an Assessment Model: Coordination, Consultation and Compromise

Robert A. Sweatman

Illinois College, a selective, residential liberal arts college founded in 1829 in Jacksonville, Illinois, enrolls about 1,000 undergraduate students. The college initiated its first graduate program in the fall of 2011. This master's (MAEd) program is designed to accommodate the professional development needs of teachers within the service region and, especially, those teachers who supervise Illinois College's undergraduate teacher preparation candidates in student teaching placements. The scope and sequence of courses was planned to provide graduate students with the knowledge and skills to effectively respond to the needs of 21st century learners and to be teacher leaders in their respective schools. The first cohort graduated during the fall 2013 semester.

Illinois College was part of Cohort Three in the Higher Learning Commission's (HLC) Pathways Initiative for reaccreditation. In fulfillment of the quality improvement component of reaccreditation, institutions in this cohort were asked to pilot the Degree Qualifications Profile (DQP). In my current position of executive director for institutional research, planning and assessment, I was assigned the role of leading the project team, and I teach a measurement course in the master's program. Although the DQP was also piloted in two of the college's undergraduate programs, this chapter references experiences associated with implementation within the MAEd program, where institutional research (IR) was most directly involved.

The challenges that necessitated assessment coordination for the DQP pilot in this program were the program's very recent inception, the

New Directions for Institutional Research, no. 165 © 2015 Wiley Periodicals, Inc.
Published online in Wiley Online Library (wileyonlinelibrary.com) • DOI: 10.1002/ir.20123

significant dispersion of the program's faculty members across academic departments (that is, psychology, sociology, communication, education, and content areas), and the technical aspects of rubric development, scoring and aggregation of results.

The overarching framework for the program's assessment of student learning is the DQP, with its five outcome areas: (a) specialized knowledge; (b) broad, integrative knowledge; (c) intellectual skills; (d) applied learning; and (e) civic learning (Lumina Foundation, 2011). Teaching-specific outcomes are concentrated in the areas of specialized knowledge and applied learning but are related to all five outcome areas.

When institutional researchers are assigned the large-scale task of coordinating assessment initiatives involving faculty from multiple disciplines, they can find themselves with limited leverage to usher these busy faculty members toward timely and technically sound implementation. As will be evident throughout this chapter, the implementation process can benefit from an IR coordinator being available as a consultant and flexible facilitator. In that role, the IR coordinator can begin by impressing upon faculty members the need for ongoing commitments of time and effort and then coordinate the execution of a well-conceived plan with some carefully measured compromises.

The Plan for Coordinating the DQP Assessment Process

The plan for coordinating the DQP assessment process involved the activities listed next in sequential order, with some reiterations and limited practical deviations. Rubrics were at the center of our efforts to promote accurate assessments of student proficiency levels for each of the DQP outcomes. Assessment of student products and performances ranged from scoring embedded extended-response test items to rating essays, papers, projects and presentations. The activities in which we engaged were as follows:

- *Introducing the DQP* assessment model to program faculty members
- *Curriculum mapping* to determine alignment of the DQP with our current program
- *Development of rubrics* for assessment of student performance related to DQP outcomes
- *Applying rubrics* to measure student proficiency
- Rubric *norming*
- Investigating *reliability* and *validity*
- *Analyzing* rubric ratings for evidence of student learning
- *Summarizing* assessment results and circulating reports
- *Acting* on assessment results

Considering the amount of cooperation that would be needed from so many busy faculty members to successfully implement this protocol, an administrator needed to remind me more than once not to let the pursuit of perfection become the enemy of progress (a sentiment often attributed to Churchill). Similarly, it was some consolation that Baartman, Bastiaens, Kirschner, and Van der Vleuten (2007) assert that each assessment does not have to meet all psychometric criteria if the use of a combination of methods for program assessment collectively meets the most important quality criteria related to the judgment to be made about student performance. This assertion was particularly comforting considering that the IR function at a college has many roles to fulfill other than assessment coordinator on a single project, and beginning with an unrealistic expectation of ensuring rigid adherence to the protocol would have been overwhelming. To further explain, the Office of IR at Illinois College supports all administrative and academic divisions of the college, yet it has only one full-time researcher, two student workers, and an intern to complete its regular tasks of internal and external reporting and to make its contributions to special projects such as the present one.

Introducing the DQP Assessment Model to Program Faculty Members. For the regularly scheduled monthly meeting of the graduate committee, composed of faculty teaching in the program and the program director, I requested that an introduction to the DQP be included on the agenda. After circulating material about the DQP, I explained the HLC quality improvement project requirements and then provided an overview of the DQP. Although a committee member offered the typical faculty bristle at what he referred to as another externally prescribed assessment tool, it was not difficult to redirect any very general critiques of the DQP's appropriateness by asking for specific examples to illustrate any misgivings.

Compelling everyone to make a commitment to participate in a thorough rubric development and refinement process was a little more challenging. Even so, it was difficult for anyone to argue convincingly against any of the previously listed basic steps that were proposed to ensure that we conduct an accurate assessment of learning in our new program. To my surprise, by the end of the meeting all in attendance had shared some positive perceptions of individual DQP outcomes, and we attained a general consensus that the tool seemed appropriate for our purposes. All committee members had even acknowledged that they would have at least some role in its application for program assessment. Actual implementation, though, brought some anticipated and unanticipated challenges, as the role of IR had to fluctuate between coordinator, consultant, and facilitator.

Curriculum Mapping to Determine Alignment of the DQP with Our Current Program. Our pilot began with curricular mapping as suggested in the Lumina Foundation's (2014) overview document on the DQP. Although it is important to know how students' proficiency levels have changed over time, it is arguably most important to ensure that students have a chance to demonstrate mastery of all intended master's-level outcomes near the end of their program. A curricular mapping document voluntarily drafted by a faculty member who reviewed the assignments described in course syllabi provided an important frame of reference for a baseline of assessment coverage of DQP outcomes, from which the faculty in the program could build. This curricular mapping matrix (DQP outcomes in rows and courses in columns) showed the high degree of alignment of the curriculum with the DQP and that all of the outcomes were addressed in more than one course, by multiple assessments, and from early to late in the program. This uncontrived alignment went a long way in marshaling faculty support for use of the DQP, as they realized that most of the assignments needed to assess performance on the DQP outcomes were already embedded in their original course designs.

For the master's degree, the capstone project and presentation provided a convenient culminating product and performance for demonstrating many of the DQP outcomes just prior to program completion. However, the master's program at Illinois College lacks the additional benefit of having a comprehensive examination that would provide an excellent opportunity for students to demonstrate outcomes within the specialized knowledge DQP category related to the major theories, developments and challenges in the field. Several faculty members realized that their assignments originally identified as opportunities to assess attainment of particular DQP outcomes needed to be modified to have more depth or breadth (for example, reflection or interdisciplinary components) to fully address the knowledge and skills referenced in the DQP. In some cases, additional assignments needed to be developed to address minor gaps in assessment coverage within the original program curriculum. The mapping process was also a very helpful starting point for identifying which faculty members had assignments that addressed the same DQP outcomes and, therefore, could collaborate on rubric development.

The Development of Rubrics for Assessment of Performance Related to DQP Outcomes.   IR assessment coordinators must be willing to become involved with the technical details of individual rubrics when necessary, yet they are often the only people involved in a project with an overarching purview to ensure that the collective coverage of the rubrics thoroughly addresses all of the targeted program outcomes. At Illinois College, coordination at the stage of rubric development oscillated from a high level of direct involvement to having only secondhand knowledge of some rubric development activities. Most of the faculty members involved with this project were experienced with developing rubrics for use in their disciplines, so when IR intervention was needed it was mainly to strike a balance between specificity and generality for program assessment purposes and in some cases with attaining continuity from high to low performance level descriptors.

In many cases, rather than having in-person meetings, one faculty member would take the initial responsibility for developing a rubric for assessment related to a particular DQP outcome and then simply forward the draft version to her or his colleague for refinement. IR was not always consulted, nor was there an expectation that it would be. Some faculty were already quite adept with rubric development, and there were instances where clear expertise in an area made it obvious which faculty member would take the lead on rubric development for a particular outcome (for example, a communication professor addressing a communication fluency outcome). However, beyond consideration of expertise and experience with rubric development, at times an IR coordinator may have to assign a faculty member as a point person on a rubric development team, simply because they can be relied upon to develop a draft rubric in a timely manner to start the team's rubric refinement process.

Though some of our faculty members assumed that they had to develop a holistic rubric for program assessment because of the need for a rubric that is sufficiently general to assess different assignments across classes, it could be argued that the compound nature of the DQP outcomes calls for analytic rubrics with multiple criteria to address each component of the outcome. Further, Zimmaro (2004) asserts that analytic rubrics tend to yield higher interrater reliability coefficients (as cited in Stellmack, Konheim-Kalkstein, Manor, Massey, & Schmitz, 2009). A balance between the general and specific can be achieved by constructing analytic rubrics that are not overly specific to particular assignments. As Jonsson and Svingby (2007) point out, "the reliability of an assessment can always, in theory, be raised to acceptable levels by providing tighter restrictions to the assessment format" (p. 136) and they recognize the role of rubrics in helping to do so; however, they also emphasize the need to avoid losing the authenticity of the assessment in the process by making rubrics too detailed. Delandshere and Petrosky (1998) note that this loss of authenticity can occur when a rater's focus shifts from interpreting performance quality to merely looking for selected traits listed in a rubric (as cited in Moskal & Leydens, 2000). The tightening up of rubrics to the point of making them assignment specific at the expense of criterion-general can compromise their usefulness for assessing the same outcome on a different assignment and thus aggregation to a higher level (DQP-criterion level or programmatic level). One solution to this dilemma, albeit at the expense of complicating program-level aggregation and analysis, is to add some assignment-specific criteria to the original program rubric. Then, when consolidating assessment results, IR must recalculate rubric total scores by excluding scores on the added criteria prior to aggregation and analysis, so that the scores will be comparable to those from other users of the unaltered original rubric that were generated from its application to other assignments. This need for comparability is critical when analyzing scores for the same student over time to determine the extent of student growth at different assessment points, as a student makes progress toward program completion.

The piloting of rubrics can begin with applying draft versions of the rubrics to existing student assignments that span a variety of proficiency levels, from novice to intermediate to mastery. With respect to the pilot project at Illinois College, some courses had not yet been offered at the time that rubrics were being developed, so student products were not yet available for all DQP outcomes. These rubrics had to be honed as the courses were offered and the respective assignments were collected and rated. Some of our initial rubrics addressed all levels (associate's, bachelor's, and master's) for a DQP outcome area, whereas others addressed only the master's level. The initial choice of which levels to address in a rubric was dependent upon the anticipated proficiency of students in each outcome area at program entry, but some rubrics were eventually altered to address only master's-level outcomes or to include bachelor's-level outcomes once incoming students' proficiency levels became evident.

To ensure that rubrics provide the collective curricular coverage for program assessment and are of high quality, it is important to have a centralized location for submitting the rubrics and a thorough framework for reviewing and critiquing them to enhance quality. The IR coordinator can run each rubric through Arter and Chappuis' (2007, p. 183) "Rubric for Rubrics" criteria to generate substantive and detailed feedback for rubric development teams for another layer of refinement. Additionally, from Jonsson and Svingby's (2007) meta-analytical study of the use of scoring rubrics, the recommendations listed here can be considered when creating and refining rubrics to enhance the reliability of their scores. The original sources cited in Jonsson and Svingby's article are included for readers who would like to conduct a more in-depth review of particular recommendations.

1. Benchmarks are most likely to increase agreement, but they should be chosen with care because the scoring depends heavily on the benchmarks chosen to define the rubric (Denner, Salzman, & Harris, 2002; Popp, Ryan, Thompson, & Behrens, 2003).

2. Analytical scoring is often preferable (Johnson, Penny, & Gordon, 2000, 2001; Penny, Johnson, & Gordon, 2000a, 2000b), but perhaps not so if the separate dimension scores are summarized in the end (Waltman, Kahn, & Koency, 1998).

3. Agreement is improved by training, but training will probably never totally eliminate differences (Stuhlmann, Daniel, Dellinger, Denny, & Powers, 1999; Weigle, 1999).

4. Topic-specific rubrics are likely to produce more generalizable and dependable scores than generic rubrics (DeRemer, 1998; Marzano, 2002).

5. Augmentation of the rating scale (for example, that the raters can expand the number of levels using + or − signs) seems to improve certain aspects of interrater reliability, although not consensus agreements (Myford, Johnson, Wilkins, Persky, & Michaels, 1996; Penny et al., 2000a, 2000b). For high levels of consensus agreement, a two-level scale (for example competent–not competent performance) can

be reliably scored with minimal training, whereas a four-level scale is more difficult to use (Williams & Rink, 2003).

6. Two raters are, under restrained conditions, enough to produce acceptable levels of interrater agreement (Baker, Abedi, Linn, & Niemi, 1995; Marzano, 2002).

Applying Rubrics to Measure Student Proficiency.   At Illinois College, IR tried not to be too prescriptive in terms of the measurement process used by faculty, as long as it appeared that their process would lead to usable assessment data. Some instructors applied the same rubric for assessment as for grading an assignment and then converted points from ratings to grades (see chapter five in Arter & Chappuis, 2007, p. 109 for instructions). Alternatively, some faculty elected to review the student product a second time after grading to apply rubric ratings explicitly for program assessment purposes.

In a couple of instances during our pilot project, descriptors for a commonly used criterion were slightly modified by faculty members to fit specific assignments, which rendered aggregation of ratings across those raters suspect. Such types of tailored modifications were an exception, and most often uniform measurement practices yielded actionable assessment data.

Overall, the array of rubrics applied to student products was quite diverse. To explain, the graduate committee had not decided to require student attainment of the DQP's conceptualization of master's-level proficiency to graduate, so all of the rubrics' rating options included more than a threshold elucidated by pass/fail descriptors. Instead, rubrics for assignments addressing different outcomes had varied numbers of points on their scales and widely varied levels of details to guide raters. Some rubrics were holistic and others analytic. Despite these differences in rubrics, as long as the descriptors for a particular criterion remained the same across instructors' rubrics when applied to the same students over time, aggregation longitudinally and to the program level was possible.

Rubric Norming.   Holmes and Oakleaf (2013) contend that "to achieve consistent and reliable use of a rubric among numerous raters, and to create the best possible tool with which to examine student work, the rubric and the raters must go through a 'norming' process" (p. 599). They provide several recommendations for norming facilitators to follow in their efforts to help their colleagues reach a consensus when rating samples of student work. A selection of some of their most salient tips for facilitators follows:

- Esteem the raters' perceptions of student performance above their own perceptions.
- "[A]llow raters to take ownership of the rubric and the scoring process" (p. 600).

- Remind raters to consider the assessment needs of the overall program over their personal assessment needs.
- Assist the raters in efforts to "identify patterns of consistency and inconsistency" in their scores (Maki, 2004; as cited in Holmes & Oakleaf, 2013, p. 601).
- Adhere to rubric best practices, such as those described by Arter and Chappuis (2007).
- Allow discussions of instructional strategies and content during the norming process.
- Remind raters that "ultimately, norming rubrics leads to reliable and valid assessment—and using reliable and valid assessments is the key to producing believable and actionable results" (p. 602).

More specific to norming procedures than these general recommendations for facilitators, Maki (2004, p. 127) outlines a concise list of six sequential steps in the rubric norming process, a review of which could benefit raters as well as the facilitator as they work toward achieving a common understanding of the criteria and ratings. It is worth noting that in most cases in the pilot project, only two or three raters needed to reach a consensus, because only the faculty members who were rating assignments that addressed a particular outcome had to calibrate their respective ratings and most DQP outcomes matched with only a couple of course-embedded assignments. Nonetheless, the norming process for our new program was quite lengthy and was somewhat disjointed compared to the tightly coupled steps recommended here and by Maki, as student products only became available to be rated when each course was taught for the first time over a 2-year period.

Methodological Considerations for IR: Investigating Reliability and Validity. Shortly after learning that I would be coordinating the process of rubric development for piloting the DQP at Illinois College, I found it helpful to reference a meta-analytical article by Jonsson and Svingby (2007) that summarizes study findings on establishing the reliability and validity of rubric scores. In an ideal world with an infinite amount of time, expertise, and resources, the reliability statistics described in that article would be fully assessed for every set of rubric scores, and each rubric would be refined until its scores reached an acceptable level of reliability for all relevant student subgroups across all raters. However, with the real-world limitations on time, expertise, and resources at Illinois College, as on most campuses, one has to move forward with the intent of forthright implementation but with a willingness to make reasoned compromises where necessitated by these limitations.

Interrater and Intrarater Reliability. Especially where the decisions to be made are between mastery and nonmastery at program culmination, it is critical to establish the percentage agreement in classification by at least two raters for each outcome of interest. Even when the decision is not as high stakes and involves assigning ratings among several performance levels, it is important to establish an acceptable level of rater consensus. According to Crocker and Algina (1986), indications of consensus typically include inter-rater correlations, intra-class correlations (for example, Cronbach's alpha for more than two judges), and the percentage of exact agreement or adjacent agreement (within one point) across raters (as cited in Stemler, 2004). Ideally, one would also determine the proportion of agreement attained beyond what is expected by chance. This analysis can be accomplished by running a Cohen's kappa using the crosstabs function in SPSS or manually calculated. Researchers have called for a Cohen's kappa of at least .40 to be considered fair agreement beyond chance (Stoddart, Abrams, Gasper, & Canaday, 2000). For determining intrarater reliability, in most cases these same measures of consistency can be applied to scores assigned by the same rater for the same student product at different points in time (that is, re-rating) (Stellmack et al., 2009). Applying data analytics associated with generalizability theory and a many-facets Rasch model to explain the components of scores (such as by types/sources of variation) are additional approaches to assessing the reliability of rubric scores that are mentioned in the literature, but both can require additional software (for example, GENOVA and FACETS, respectively) to assist with the computations (Jonsson & Svingby, 2007). Target values for many of the above-referenced reliability statistics are provided in the article by Jonsson and Svingby (2007).

Establishing Internal Consistency Reliability. In their article about establishing reliability, MacLaughlin, Fike, Alvarez, Seifert, and Blaszczyk (2010) assert that demonstrating internal consistency reliability across item scores for the criteria within a rubric is a necessary condition for establishing construct validity for a set of rubric scores. They used Cronbach's alpha as their measure of internal consistency to provide evidence that the items in their rubric consistently measured students' performance on their construct of interest. Conceptually, the alpha reliability coefficient value is an indication of "the proportion of observed score variance that is attributable to true scores" (Traub & Rowley, 1991, p. 42). Technically, with respect to rubric scores, the coefficient alpha represents the proportion of total rubric score variance that is accounted for by the systematic (true score) variance among rubric criteria scores. Looking at the remaining variance that is random and not systematic, Frisbie (1988) explains that:

> a reliability coefficient is a number that provides an index of the amount of error associated with a particular set of test scores. It can range from 1.00, indicating perfect reliability or no measurement error, down to 0.00, indicating that the presence (abundance) of random error is the only reason why students obtained scores that differed from one another. (p. 28)

When calculating an alpha coefficient in SPSS, a user can also quickly determine the alpha value with each criterion removed, which helps to identify criteria that do not correlate as strongly with the other criteria and may be considered for revision or deletion. Keep in mind that this particular use of Cronbach's alpha, as a measure of internal consistency reliability, is for examining the interrelatedness of criteria scores from an analytical rubric with its multiple criteria and cannot be used when employing a holistic rubric that has only an overall score. At Illinois College, some of our sets of rubric scores did not meet the standard of an acceptable alpha coefficient of .65 or greater for accurately estimating group-level scores. However, IR found that when calculating a separate alpha coefficient for each subset of criteria that comprised a distinct content area within a rubric, the reliability estimates for scores from these homogenous subsets were more likely to result in alpha coefficients of an acceptable level.

Building a Credible Validity Argument.   Moskal and Leydens (2000, Validity section, para. 1) assert that "Validation is the process of accumulating evidence that supports the appropriateness of the inferences that are made of student responses for specified assessment uses." They encourage instructors to already begin thinking about the valid interpretation of assessment results when they are developing assignments, noting that "a well-designed scoring rubric cannot correct for a poorly designed assessment instrument" (Validity Concerns in Rubric Development section, para. 1). Accordingly, they recommend that instructors consider what they want to know about their students (purpose) and how the students will demonstrate their abilities (objectives) to direct them as they develop their assignments and scoring rubrics. If rubrics are not effectively normed and reliability estimates for sets of rubric scores are too low, such factors undermine one's ability to make a convincing validity argument. If there are too many weaknesses of this nature in the evidence for several sets of rubric scores, the validity of the overall program assessment model may even be compromised.

Moskal and Leydens (2000) define four types of validity evidence that are relevant to the development and application of scoring rubrics and the resulting scores: content, construct, criterion, and consequential. The authors provide a series of questions that are helpful for assessing the appropriateness of a scoring rubric relative to its purpose. These questions should be asked for each draft version of a rubric before it is finalized. If an answer is "no" for a set of rubric scores, the rubric should be refined or any application of the results should be limited accordingly. In the assessment process associated with the pilot project, we were not able to answer an unequivocal "yes" to some of these questions for some of the sets of rubric scores from our program assessment, so the usefulness of the corresponding results was discounted commensurately in the assessment report.

Moskal and Leydens (2000) define content-related evidence as how well a student's responses to an assessment instrument are representative of that particular student's knowledge of the relevant content. The authors provide three questions that rubric developers should ask related to content validity including whether the criteria includes unnecessary content, addresses all elements of the content in question, and if content that should be evaluated with the rubric is all addressed by the rubric.

The authors define construct-related evidence as that which indicates that an assessment instrument is sufficiently and exclusively measuring the construct of interest. They suggest two questions that rubric developers should ask related to construct validity: is everything of interest assessed through the scoring criteria and are any criteria not aligned to the construct of interest?

Rafilson (1991) defines criterion-related evidence as that which shows that assessment results can be generalized to performance on other pertinent tasks, whereas others have referred to this type of validity evidence as demonstrating that assessment results are predictive of a pertinent event (as cited in Moskal & Leydens, 2000). Moskal and Leydens recommend that rubric developers ask four questions related to criterion validity:

1. How do the scoring criteria reflect competencies that would suggest success on future or related performance?
2. What are the important components of the future or related performance that may be evaluated through the use of the assessment instrument?
3. How do the scoring criteria measure the important components of the future or related performance?
4. Are there any facets of the future or related performance that are not reflected in the scoring criteria?

When having discussions related to these criterion-related validity questions, the Illinois College Graduate Committee noted that one important measure of future performance would be whether graduates of the program would be effective leaders of action research projects in their schools and effective communicators of their results to promote school improvement. This realization led to incorporating into the capstone project a presentation with a rubric that addressed each student's ability to effectively communicate her or his study results and the implications for practice to an audience of their school administrators and teaching colleagues who were invited to campus to attend their presentations.

Moskal and Leydens (2000) assert that gathering consequential evidence involves careful consideration of the potential consequences of using the assessment results and an attempt to identify plausible alternative explanations for the results. An example of a question that rubric developers should ask related to consequential evidence is whether application of the rubric consistently leads to disparate results for subgroups because of unrelated characteristics of the assessment. When IR disaggregates results, such disparities can be identified. However, it takes further investigation to determine whether those disparities represent bias in the instrument design or its application or whether the difference in ratings truly represents actual subgroup differences in the skills or knowledge that are intended to be measured.

Analyzing Rubric Ratings for Evidence of Student Learning.   In the pilot project, scored rubrics were gathered by the IR office and the ratings were entered at the student level into an SPSS database. It is important that the data are entered in this unit-level manner, which allows the analyst to study individual student performance and group performance on DQP outcomes at the first point of measurement and at multiple points along the path to program completion. IR can create aggregate reports that summarize changes in performance over time, across raters, within courses, within performance areas, and overall, including the percentages of graduates who achieved each degree of master's-level proficiency on all DQP outcomes by program completion.

Some preliminary findings associated with this pilot project prompted follow-up with individual instructors, as some students were rated more highly on an outcome indicator earlier in the program than they were later in the program. What at first seemed counterintuitive was easily explained, as different types of assignments to measure performance on different aspects of the same outcome can yield different results without either assessment being faulty and even without a student actually regressing. To the extent that both assessments are found to be valid, each can provide valuable evidence of an aspect of achievement even if the results for an indicator are ostensibly inconsistent.

Consumers of the initial program assessment report tend to generate requests for more in-depth analysis of results that require integration with data elements from other databases (for example, SIS data that includes demographic and other pre-program-entry characteristics). For our pilot project, one such request pertained to a comparison of performance levels for alums of Illinois College's undergraduate teacher preparation program with the performance levels of students from other undergraduate programs. Other requests involved comparisons of the performance of student groups by undergraduate cumulative grade point average intervals, by years of teaching experience intervals, and by the class levels in which students are certified to teach.

Summarize Assessment Results and Circulate Reports.   At Illinois College, all programs are required to summarize assessment results in a report to the dean of the college and to the assessment committee. This report must have descriptions of the following components: learning goals, targets, multiple assessment methods, results, implications, and action plans. In instances where technical rigor is compromised to some extent during the assessment process, the last line of defense for the report writer is to include qualifying statements in the overall assessment report that address the implications of the compromise on the interpretation of results. Despite acknowledged compromises, the assessment report for the Illinois College MAEd program was highlighted by the assessment committee as being indicative of a well-designed and implemented assessment model and was circulated for other departments on campus to reference.

Perhaps the most useful assessment reports are less formal and circulated at the departmental level. Maki (2004) suggests that "results presented narratively accompanied by quantitative analyses of student performance based on scoring rubrics provide two ways for groups to identify patterns of strong and weak performance" (p. 160). At Illinois College, such patterns were identified when smaller scale reports that summarize disaggregated data were created by IR to answer specific questions from the graduate committee, program faculty members and from the MAEd program director. Most of the smaller follow-up reports prompted further conversations among faculty members that helped to answer what Maki (2004) refers to as the most important question about assessment results: "Why?"

Acting on Assessment Results.   The most important test of the effectiveness of the assessment process described here is whether the various activities led to instruments and practices that generated actionable information to improve the program. In our pilot project, despite deviations from the original protocol described, including some rubrics not being systematically refined or normed, clear patterns on strengths and weaknesses by criterion and DQP outcome were identified that led to curricular changes from the individual assignment level (for example, address particular foundational bachelor's-level outcomes with preliminary assignments as precursors to master's-level outcomes, particularly for quantitative fluency) to the program level (for example, change in the sequence of courses for future cohorts).

Examples of Changes.   An examination of outcomes related to the DQP Intellectual Skills area of quantitative fluency provides an example of how the graduate committee at Illinois College is determining the programmatic implications of assessment findings that were obtained at multiple points in the program. Proficiency with quantitative fluency relative to expectations at all degree levels was assessed several times within a course titled, "Measurement in Education" and was subsequently assessed by rating student performance on the results section of each student's capstone paper submitted at program completion. Ideally, the quantitative-related assessment results would have shown consistent student growth from the beginning to the end of the course and ultimately would have indicated a high level of student quantitative proficiency in the program's culminating capstone project. However, the course-level assessment results alerted the instructor to a concern about the ability of one-third of the students to successfully apply the quantitative approaches learned in class to their own datasets for a major course project. Upon review of the aggregated assessment results at the program-level, IR reported to the graduate committee that rubric ratings suggested an inability for this same group of students to accurately interpret their study results when completing their capstone action research projects at program completion. The lack of demonstrated growth with respect to this skill set that is critical for graduate students' success called for a programmatic response.

The graduate committee decided that future students identified as struggling in this area would need to be assigned an advisor familiar with quantitative work, and that the instructor for the research methodology course would need to work closely with such students and their capstone project advisors as students planned the data analysis component of their capstone projects. This intensified guidance will be particularly important to move such students toward successful project completion, because assessment results revealed that some students tend to rely on DQP bachelor's-degree-level, step-by-step instructions to analyze their data and to interpret their results, and the imperfect data from field studies rarely are amenable to such formulaic protocols. Further, just as review sessions on quantitative analysis techniques were offered throughout the measurement course, it became evident that they also were needed near the end of the program when capstone projects necessitated recollection of data analysis techniques and the skillful interpretation of results.

Because retention of quantitative knowledge and skills was found to be lacking for some students even from the beginning to the end of a single course on measurement, it is no wonder that some struggled to apply quantitative techniques on their projects near program completion. IR recommended to the graduate committee that quantitative content should be interwoven and reinforced where most appropriate in some of the earlier coursework in the program. Specific suggestions included guided reviews of the methodology and results sections of research articles in the cognitive development and instructional communication courses and more quantitative requirements in the research paper assignments in these early courses.

Conclusion

Lessons were learned about IR coordination of assessment efforts at each step in the process of piloting the DQP. Foremost among the lessons was the need to balance the assessment data-related needs of the program with the interests of faculty and students. To strike this balance, an IR coordinator of an assessment initiative should not hesitate to compromise when it does not substantially jeopardize the integrity of the assessment, as not all aspects of the assessment protocol are equally critical to ensuring the reliability and validity of the overall assessment initiative or even of individual sets of rubric ratings. An example of such an acceptable compromise is when a rubric developer does not initially have a faculty partner with whom to collaborate on rubric norming because another faculty member in the program has not yet been identified as a potential user of the same rubric. Less formal rubric norming can be accomplished by asking a colleague in a similar discipline to rate some student products (preferably at different performance levels) with the rubric for scoring comparison purposes, to see if a general scoring consensus can be reached. Talking through rationales for the assignment of ratings can lead to greater between- and within-rater consistency because raters tend to be more intentional in the assignment of ratings when they have articulated their thoughts on the specific characteristics of the various performance levels for a criterion. The acceptability of such a compromise with respect to the formality of the norming process is supported by the research of Bresciani et al. (2009). These researchers found that faculty ratings from a rubric developed to measure research quality across a variety of disciplines from undergraduate to graduate studies achieved an acceptable level of agreement without undergoing a formal norming process, and they attributed this to the rich discussions during rubric development that served an informal norming function.

To prepare for the formal rubric development and norming process, it was helpful to read the relevant articles cited in this chapter and to consult with faculty members in the Illinois College teacher preparation program who had a wealth of experience with rubrics. I had the additional benefit of recently teaching an educational measurement course, which addressed the reliability and validity of rubric scores.

Even if an IR assessment coordinator cannot oversee the full execution of all recommended protocols, communicating to team members the conditions associated with the valid use of scores and what each reliability statistic is intended to represent improves discernment in the approach to rubric construction and refinement. Such discussions between IR and faculty of validity and reliability concerns help to give direction and purpose to the rubric development process.

By starting with a comprehensive framework for program assessment, conscious decisions can be made as to what to forego due to limitations in resources. At Illinois College we found that a few practical deviations, acts of omission and commission, from our ambitious initial protocol only limited the use of any tenuous sets of scores but did not jeopardize the integrity of the overall process. When an IR coordinator has the benefit of an assessment model that aligns well with the existing curriculum, a detailed plan for ensuring a sufficient measure of quality control with respect to the development of rubrics and one that allows for faculty ownership of embedded assessments, actionable information about student learning can be generated despite some shortcomings in adherence to all of the technical aspects of plan implementation.

Since the initial pilot, the Illinois College MAEd program has continued to use the DQP outcomes as the foundation for its program assessment. In its most recently submitted assessment report, the DQP served as the primary reference for the rubrics developed to assess the performance of the spring 2015 graduating class.

New Directions for Institutional Research • DOI: 10.1002/ir

References

Arter, J., & Chappuis, J. (2007). *Creating & recognizing quality rubrics.* New Jersey: Pearson Education.

Baartman, L. K. J., Bastiaens, T. J., Kirschner, P. A., & Van der Vleuten, C. P. M. (2007). Assessment in competence-based education: How can assessment quality be evaluated? *Educational Research Review, 2*(2), 114–129. doi: 10.1016/j.edurev.2007.06.001

Baker, E. L., Abedi, J., Linn, R. L., & Niemi, D. (1995). Dimensionality and generalizability of domain-independent performance assessments. *Journal of Educational Research, 89,* 197–205.

Bresciani, M. J., Oakleaf, M., Kolkhorst, F., Nebeker, C., Barlow, J., Duncan, K., et al. (2009). Examining design and inter-rater reliability of a rubric measuring research quality across multiple disciplines. *Practical Assessment, Research, & Evaluation, 14*(12), 1–7.

Crocker, L., & Algina, J. (1986). *Introduction to classical and modern test theory.* Philadelphia, PA: Harcourt Brace Jovanovich College Publishers.

Delandshere, G., & Petrosky, A. (1998). Assessment of complex performances: Limitations of key measurement assumptions. *Educational Research, 27*(2), 14–24.

Denner, P. R., Salzman, S. A., & Harris, L. B. (2002, February). *Teacher work sample assessment: An accountability method that moves beyond teacher testing to the impact of teacher performance on student learning.* Paper presented at the annual meeting of the American Association of Colleges for Teacher Education, New York, NY.

DeRemer, M. L. (1998). Writing assessment: Raters' elaboration of the rating task. *Assessing Writing, 5,* 7–29.

Frisbie, D. A. (1988). Reliability of scores from teacher-made tests. *Educational Measurement: Issues and Practice, 7,* 25–35. doi:10.1111/j.1745-3992.1988.tb00422.x

Holmes, C., & Oakleaf, M. (2013). The official (and unofficial) rules for norming rubrics successfully. *Journal of Academic Librarianship, 39*(6), 599–602. doi: 10.1016/j.acalib.2013.09.001

Johnson, R. L., Penny, J., & Gordon, B. (2000). The relation between score resolution methods and interrater reliability: An empirical study of an analytic scoring rubric. *Applied Measurement in Education, 13,* 121–138.

Johnson, R. L., Penny, J., & Gordon, B. (2001). Score resolution and the interrater reliability of holistic scores in rating essays. *Written Communication, 18,* 229–249.

Jonsson, A., & Svingby, G. (2007). The use of scoring rubrics: Reliability, validity and educational consequences. *Educational Research Review, 2*(2), 130–144. doi: 10.1016/j.edurev.2007.05.002

Lumina Foundation for Education. (2011). *The Degree Qualifications Profile.* Indianapolis, IN: Author.

Lumina Foundation for Education. (2014). *The Degree Qualifications Profile* (2nd ed.). Indianapolis, IN: Author.

MacLaughlin, E. J., Fike, D. S., Alvarez, C. A., Seifert, C. F., & Blaszczyk, A. T. (2010). Reliability of a seminar grading rubric in a grand rounds course. *Journal of Multidisciplinary Healthcare. 3,* 169–179. Published online 2010 Sep 9. doi:10.2147/JMDH.S12346.

Maki, P. L. (2004). *Assessing for learning: Building a sustainable commitment across the institution.* Sterling, VA: Stylus.

Marzano, R. J. (2002). A comparison of selected methods of scoring classroom assessments. *Applied Measurement in Education, 15,* 249–267.

Moskal, B. M., & Leydens, J. (2000). Scoring rubric development: Validity and reliability. *Practical Assessment Research and Evaluation, 7*(10). Retrieved from http://pareonline.net/getvn.asp?v=7&n=10.

Myford, C. M., Johnson, E., Wilkins, R., Persky, H., & Michaels, M. (1996, April). *Constructing scoring rubrics: Using "facets" to study design features of descriptive rating scales.* Paper presented at the annual meeting of the American Educational Research Association, New York, NY.

Penny, J., Johnson, R. L., & Gordon, B. (2000a). The effect of rating augmentation on inter-rater reliability: An empirical study of a holistic rubric. *Assessing Writing, 7,* 143–164.

Penny, J., Johnson, R. L., & Gordon, B. (2000b). Using rating augmentation to expand the scale of an analytic rubric. *Journal of Experimental Education, 68,* 269–287.

Popp, S. E. O., Ryan, J. M., Thompson, M. S., & Behrens, J. T. (2003, April). *Operationalizing the rubric: The effect of benchmark selection on the assessed quality of writing.* Paper presented at Annual Meeting of the American Educational Research Association, Chicago, IL.

Rafilson, F. (1991). The case for validity generalization. *Practice Assessment, Research & Evaluation, 2*(13). Retrieved from http://PAREonline.net/getvn.asp?v=2--2&n=2013.

Stellmack, M. A., Konheim-Kalkstein, Y. L., Manor, J. E., Massey, A. R., & Schmitz J. A. P. (2009). An assessment of reliability and validity of a rubric for grading APA-style introductions. *Teaching of Psychology, 36*(2), 102–107. doi: 10.1080/00986280902739776

Stemler, S. E. (2004). A comparison of consensus, consistency, and measurement approaches to estimating interrater reliability. *Practical Assessment, Research & Evaluation, 9*(4). Retrieved from http://pareonline.net/getvn.asp?v=9&n=4.

Stoddart, T., Abrams, R., Gasper, E., & Canaday, D. (2000). Concept maps as assessment in science inquiry learning: A report of methodology. *International Journal of Science Education, 22,* 1221–1246. doi: 10.1080/095006900750036235

Stuhlmann, J., Daniel, C., Dellinger, A., Denny, R. K., & Powers, T. (1999). A generalizability study of the effects of training on teachers' abilities to rate children's writing using a rubric. *Journal of Reading Psychology, 20,* 107–127.

Traub, R. E., & Rowley, G. L. (1991). Understanding reliability. *Educational Measurement: Issues and Practice, 10,* 37–45. doi: 10.1111/j.1745-3992.1991.tb00183.x

Waltman, K., Kahn, A., & Koency, G. (1998). *Alternative approaches to scoring: The effects of using different scoring methods on the validity of scores from a performance assessment* (CSE Technical Report 488). Los Angeles: Center for the Study of Evaluation, University of California-Los Angeles.

Weigle, S. C. (1999). Investigating rater/prompt interactions in writing assessment: Quantitative and qualitative approaches. *Assessing Writing, 6,* 145–178.

Williams, L., & Rink, J. (2003). Teacher competency using observational scoring rubrics. *Journal of Teaching in Physical Education, 22,* 552–572.

Zimmaro, D.M. (2004). *Developing grading rubrics.* Retrieved from http://www.utexas.edu/academic/mec/research/pdf/rubricshandout.pdf

Robert A. Sweatman is the executive director for institutional research, planning and assessment at Illinois College, and he teaches a course in educational measurement in the college's MAEd program.

5

Pulling together work on the DQP and Tuning, the author presents four possible frameworks to view engagement with the DQP using the case of transfer and faculty development as examples along with four potential dilemmas IR offices may face when undertaking work with the DQP.

The DQP in Practice: A Framework of Dilemmas Facing Institutional Researchers in Community Colleges

Sandra Fulton Bath

The Degree Qualifications Profile (DQP), as described earlier in this volume, is a consensus framework of degree-level proficiencies that provides a profile of what students should know and be able to do in order to earn the associate, bachelor's, and master's degrees in any field of study (Lumina Foundation, 2011). As such, the DQP has been a siren's call to those who would have their stakeholders understand what a degree demands and what it means. As seductive as the DQP rhetoric is, however, clear images of DQP-aligned curricula, instructional activities, and assessment plans for specific fields of study often remain too idealized to be useful to those responsible for documenting and enhancing student learning at the program/department and institutional levels. Tuning efforts, coordinated by the Institute for Evidence-Based Change (IEBC), are helping program heads and other teaching faculty make the perilous leap from consensus framework to field-specific learning outcomes expected by relevant employers and faculty at receiving institutions of higher learning (Jankowski & Marshall, 2014).

This chapter aims to facilitate Tuning efforts undertaken at community colleges by those responsible for assembling program-level, evidence-centered accounts of student learning. It begins by characterizing the DQP as a *consensus framework* and differentiating it from the normative, theoretical, and practical frameworks that respectively guide curricular mapping, program-level assessment of student learning outcomes, and the maintenance of productive relationships among program heads and institutional researchers at Reynolds Community College and beyond.

New Directions for Institutional Research, no. 165 © 2015 Wiley Periodicals, Inc.
Published online in Wiley Online Library (wileyonlinelibrary.com) • DOI: 10.1002/ir.20124

Each section first describes the hallmarks of the framework—consensus, normative, theoretical, or practical—and explains how that type of framework is relevant to DQP and Tuning efforts. The chapter works through each framework to describe each, including the sources of evidence that inform the frameworks. The chapter then discusses the implications for associate degree programs of various types and conclude by examining the implications for assembling DQP-aligned curricula and assessment plans in community colleges. The chapter draws upon observations and experiences vetting the DQP with program heads and other teaching faculty during the course of faculty development workshops conducted between May 2012 and June 2014.

Finally, the chapter adds a fifth framework to those noted previously—a *framework of dilemmas* facing institutional researchers attempting to assess DQP proficiencies at the associate degree level. I will argue that similar types of dilemmas—conceptual, developmental, cultural, and political—arise when attempting to create program-specific curricula and assessment protocols aligned with the DQP, highlighting the special challenges associated with doing this work in community colleges.

A Consensus Framework

The DQP provides a set of reference points for what students should know and be able to do to earn the associate, bachelor's, and master's degrees, regardless of discipline or domain of expertise. Developed through dialogue and information exchange, it represents a confluence of evidence from empirical research, practical wisdom, and ideological belief. Collectively, those who endorse it signal to the world a mutual commitment to ensuring the quality of academic credentials at each level and acknowledge a shared responsibility for making degree qualifications transparent to those inside higher education and to the public at large.

As a *consensus* framework, the DQP describes and circumscribes a set of interrelated student proficiencies as a set of common commitments and collective responsibilities. These proficiencies are classified according to five categories: specialized knowledge, broad and integrative knowledge, intellectual skills, applied and collaborative learning, and civic and global learning (Lumina Foundation, 2011). However, because it is a consensus framework and not a *theoretical* framework, the DQP does not specify a set of rules for determining whether local, program-specific learning outcomes represent legitimate instances of these categories or proficiencies. Neither does it represent a *practical* framework, to be evaluated for its utility across fields of study. Rather, in a way, it is a *normative* framework, specifying repertoires of proficiencies from which graduates might selectively demonstrate the qualifications that warrant their degrees.

The DQP has no formal signatories, as some other consensus frameworks do. Nevertheless, it is meant to be endorsed *voluntarily*, following a

NEW DIRECTIONS FOR INSTITUTIONAL RESEARCH • DOI: 10.1002/ir

process of local vetting at the program and institutional levels. It is designed to serve as a template for drafting individualized degree profiles at the program level, and for aggregating those profiles at the institution level. It is not designed to be adopted verbatim, as a one-size-fits-all set of benchmarks; nor is it meant to override existing standards. It is simply a tool intended to highlight and reinforce existing commitments, and whenever possible, help institutions make those commitments explicit to students, faculty, administrators, and policy makers within and across institutions of higher learning and to employers and other stakeholders in local and global communities.

When beginning our DQP project, it was important for the teams to understand and agree on whether the DQP should be viewed as a consensus framework or a framework of a different sort. Working with our partner institution, Virginia Commonwealth University (VCU) made it vital to engage in shared conceptual frameworks for the work, especially around the issues of transfer. For instance, when college transfer students leave Reynolds, they are more likely to enter a bachelor's degree program at VCU than any other 4-year college, with about 74% of Reynolds transfer students going to VCU. Reynolds graduates with transfer-oriented associate's degrees are guaranteed admission to VCU with junior standing, as long as their grades are sufficient to meet the terms of the guaranteed admission agreement. The guaranteed admission agreement between the Virginia Community College System and VCU is predicated upon the commensurability of general education coursework offered at each institution. Likewise, each program articular agreement between Reynolds and VCU is predicated upon the commensurability of program-specific and general education coursework required of aspiring majors in their first two years at both institutions.

Reynolds began the project with the desire to make the argument to its stakeholders that its students are at no relative disadvantage—in terms of persistence, general success, and specific learning outcome—as compared to their freshman and sophomore peers aspiring to the same majors at VCU. Likewise, VCU needs to be able to argue that its students are acquiring the general education core competencies defined by the State Council of Higher Education for Virginia. To satisfy these arguments, our proposed Quality Collaborative sought to

1. Gauge the performance of Reynolds' aspiring transfer students against the performance of native VCU freshmen and sophomores, as enrolled in the courses designed to target common general education outcomes.
2. Gauge the performance of its former Reynolds students against the performance of native VCU students in the capstone courses for particular degree programs.
3. Ensure that students' performance in general education coursework predicts success in capstone courses equally well for native versus former Reynolds students.

Thus, the DQP project involved Reynolds selecting five courses required for transfer students enrolled in the college transfer programs and VCU selecting five courses required for native freshmen and sophomores that most closely overlap with those at Reynolds. In addition, capstone courses were selected for students graduating with a baccalaureate degree. Prior to faculty from these courses getting together for workshops, the leads on assessment examined institutional data in terms of issues of curricular coherence. The two institutions then examined, for the selected courses, the commensurability of learning objectives, intentionality of instructional activities, and utility of assessment for gauging performance in the course and with regard to DQP proficiencies. For this work to be fruitful and meaningful, it was vital for the partner institutions to determine from the outset under which frameworks they would understand the work, develop questions, and generally operate within. With agreement on the approaches, it then positions the institutions to better meet the project goals of establishing external curricular coherence, ensuring internal curriculum coherence, documenting and enhancing student learning, developing faculty as instructional designers and research partners, and documenting and enhancing faculty learning.

At Reynolds, we engaged with the DQP as a normative, consensus framework in workshops involving faculty from both Reynolds Community College and Virginia Commonwealth University. These workshops were conducted jointly by faculty development and assessment leaders from both institutions. These three workshops focused on preparing faculty who taught transferrable general education and program-specific coursework at both institutions to advance efforts with the DQP. Two additional workshops, conducted by staff at Reynolds, focused on preparing program heads and other key faculty who taught capstone courses for occupational-technical programs at Reynolds. A third Reynolds workshop focused on preparing additional faculty who taught any course required for any associate degree. Jointly conducted workshops, which served 25 faculty, were funded by the Lumina Foundation and the William and Flora Hewlett Foundation as part of the Association of American Colleges and Universities' Quality Collaboratives project (Berg et al., 2014). The remaining workshops, serving an additional 70 faculty, were funded by Reynolds Community College from surplus strategic initiative funds.

The introduction of the DQP into these workshops proved to be disruptive in the best sense of the word. It induced dilemmas that required us to reflect on the ideas, principles, and values that directed activity at our institution. Several months of this reflection made the theoretical and practical frameworks that structured activities at Reynolds stand in much sharper relief in relation to the DQP, which functioned as a consensus framework for us. Our dilemmas proved to be opportunities to refine our activities as educators.

Relationship to Tuning. At any institution of higher learning, the design and evaluation of curricula and instruction require the coordinated efforts of multiple individuals. Teaching faculty, instructional designers, faculty developers, program heads, assessment directors, research analysts, and policy leads (at various levels of organization within the institution and beyond, e.g., system, state, region) bear roles and responsibilities. It is common, even among the most differentiated and hierarchically integrated bureaucracies, for one individual to assume multiple roles in this process or for the responsibilities of several individuals to overlap. Each of these individuals provides something significant that contributes to institutional research.

For anyone who assumes a role in this coordinated effort the DQP can be introduced for vetting (or, heaven forbid, as a preendorsed *fait accompli*). As one might imagine, all manner of challenges—conceptual, developmental, cultural, and political—can arise from competing conceptions of what the DQP is, how it is designed to be used, and what its endorsement signals to the world about the purposes and collective responsibilities of higher education. Presenting the DQP as a consensus framework, subject to local vetting as a prelude to the creation of locally constructed qualifications profiles—goes a long way toward preempting some of the challenges inherent in what is, effectively, a dilemma of definition.

For instance, many involved in designing and evaluating curricula for degree programs misconstrue the DQP as a theoretical framework. They expect the DQP to capture all of the types and forms of knowledge targeted within a specific discipline or domain of expertise, and apply the syntax of their own disciplines to evaluate the legitimacy of DQP proficiencies as hallmarks of successful program graduates. If they balk at some proficiencies—or at an entire category of proficiencies—they are likely to dismiss the DQP out of hand as invalid, inapplicable, and/or biased against programs of a particular type. In such cases, presenting the DQP as a tool to be vetted, adapted, and endorsed voluntarily, as a means of highlighting shared commitments at the degree level, helps faculty focus on the network of proficiencies that distinguish their graduates from those of other programs. In some cases, proficiencies articulated in the DQP helped our educational program heads recognize their own implicit expectations and prompted them to make those expectations explicit for students and other stakeholders.

Other types of challenge arise not so much out of misconceptions of the DQP itself but from apprehensions triggered by the introduction of the DQP as a set of benchmarks to be evaluated at the program and institution levels. Even though they understand that the DQP does not prescribe how to target or assess proficiencies at the program or institution level, many faculty who vet the DQP anticipate increased demands for pedagogical content knowledge and teaching expertise arising from attempts to incorporate new DQP proficiencies into their curricula. Likewise, many assessment professionals foresee new demands for locating or developing evaluation tools that tap into DQP proficiencies, especially those that are cross-disciplinary and therefore impossible to embed in specific courses.

Faculty and staff also tend not to understand the DQP to be, in and of itself, a policy-setting document. They see that it includes no formal enforcement mechanism and no rules for determining whether a local organization is acting in accordance with the commitments to student learning specified in the framework. (Obviously, the Lumina Foundation does not intend to usurp the role of regional accreditors.) Nevertheless, it is not difficult for faculty and assessment staff to foresee how administrators at regional, state, system, and institution levels could supplement a mandated DQP with policies designed to monitor and enforce compliance. Faculty often anticipate and even experience the effects of cultures of compliance in the form of pressure to deliver "canned" courses featuring common assessments, practices which work to reduce individual autonomy, force misalignments of instructional strategies and assessments, and derail the development of professional identity among discipline-specific teaching faculty. Where the DQP aspires to encourage consistency in general proficiencies, faculty sometimes worry that the DQP is a standardizing instrument that flattens the important distinctions that define various disciplines and their necessarily different approaches to promoting learning.

The Tuning process offers a concept that tends to mitigate such anxieties among faculty. As described in the introduction to this volume, Tuning offers a process or set of principles (depending on how it is approached) for defining a particular discipline's learning. Tuning, traditionally undertaken in multi-institutional projects, emphasizes the autonomy of individual programs and their approaches to student learning even as it promotes comparability. Because Tuning encourages shared outcomes while acknowledging important differentiating factors, its principles can provide a frame for helping faculty to understand use of the DQP locally. As faculty work toward integration of the DQP's vetted proficiencies in their own curricula, Tuning acknowledges the legitimacy of disciplinary distinctions in *how* programs construct outcomes-oriented approaches to the development of those proficiencies. In other words, Tuning provides a means of addressing the DQP as a consensus framework rather than a standardizing document. If a dilemma of definitions confronted us at the outset of our work with the DQP, then the principles of Tuning enabled a productive way of defining programs' relationships to the proficiencies in the DQP.

A Normative Framework

A normative framework specifies a set of dispositions to act in accordance with specific ideological or philosophical commitments. For instance, teaching faculty are expected to uphold the values of justice, fairness, and equity. Faculty aspire to have these values guide their professional

NEW DIRECTIONS FOR INSTITUTIONAL RESEARCH • DOI: 10.1002/ir

interactions with others, not because they are empirically supported or because they work in practical terms, but because they represent the right thing to do. These commitments may be explicit, expressed in propositional form (e.g., *It is important to ensure that students understand the criteria by which their work will be judged*). More often than not, however, our moral commitments must be inferred from the stories we tell, in which we present professional dilemmas and position ourselves as moral agents, aligned with or against the values to which we aspire.

Tuning efforts currently being coordinated by IEBC are guided by an explicit normative framework. Values such as transparency, inclusion, equity, and collaboration have obvious practical benefits but also represent convictions about what constitutes the right course of action to protect the interests of more vulnerable stakeholders in the Tuning and assessment enterprise (e.g., current students, recent graduates, new and adjunct faculty). If we are to endorse the DQP as a consensus framework, we must also endorse these values as principles guiding our local work.

The ethical framework that characterizes our work at Reynolds seeks to keep faculty at the center of administrative efforts to document and enhance student learning. Community colleges—but not all associate degree-granting institutions—are nonprofit organizations that, by definition, must measure their success in terms of *changed human beings*. Our performance metrics must not only include the number of changed human beings, but estimates of the magnitude of those changes as well. In addition for institutional research, working with the DQP involves a change in the unit of analysis from examining the institution as a whole to ensuring that every student moving through our institution has opportunities and are meeting the agreed upon learning outcomes in varied ways.

Within the community college, instructors of record—the faculty members charged with designing, delivering, and evaluating course sections—are *the human change agents* of the organization. Their labor contributes directly to the bottom line, in terms of the metric that defines the success of the nonprofit. The quality of the individual course section, therefore, is the bottleneck in an educational system that seeks to maximize both the quantity and quality of its graduates. Many people agree that this is so; however, not many fully understand the implications of defining the instructor of record this way. To maximize throughput and optimize quality, all components of the system must be subverted to the bottleneck. This means that the work of all other functionaries must be subverted to the needs and capacities of *those who teach the courses*, regardless of faculty status or rank. Focusing on the development needs of instructors, increasing their capacities, becomes central to the mission of the college. Administrators must remember that, although their activities help maintain the organization, the ultimate purpose of those activities is to make high-quality instruction available to students. With such a lens in mind, the role of institutional research (IR) becomes one of providing support to enhance the teaching and learning process and working with faculty to address questions they have regarding students and their learning.

Most of our parables at Reynolds illustrate a commitment to protecting faculty in their roles as the primary *human change agents* of the organization. The following are examples of decisions we have made over the course of our DQP work that align with this commitment:

- We decided to *vet* the DQP with faculty at Reynolds, rather than present it to them as an administrator-endorsed *fait accompli*.
- We compensated workshop participants, at a contracted flat rate of $800 for 30 hours of work and specific deliverables, regardless of faculty status or rank.
- We discouraged the development of "canned courses," featuring common syllabi, lesson plans, and assessment tools, even among adjunct faculty.
- We discouraged faculty from sacrificing the alignment of their courses vis a vis each other at any cost, even when it meant sacrificing external alignment to extra-program courses.

By vetting the DQP within programs, faculty at Reynolds were able to create discipline-specific consensus, normative frameworks that were aligned to the DQP's proficiencies. These documents enable a process of mapping disciplinary versions of the DQP's proficiencies to the master document so as to create, across disciplines, a composite map of where the DQP's proficiencies are addressed across the entire campus. As noted previously, however, consensus, normative frameworks demand little more than agreement that the learning communicated should be included in curricula and pedagogies. It leaves unaddressed the more discrete knowledge and skills that comprise the proficiencies described and does little for defining how students might demonstrate their grasp of that learning in particular disciplinary contexts—thus moving us into the dilemma of measurement.

A Theoretical Framework

Our response to this dilemma was a *theoretical framework*. A theoretical framework, in contrast to a consensus framework, includes more than a set of inter-related propositions; it also includes a set of rules for determining what is and is not legitimate to say. In order to endorse a consensus framework, one need only agree that something is desirable for a given purpose. To endorse a *theoretical* framework, however, one must agree *that something is so*, and also understand *why it is so*: the grounds on which its warrants can be asserted, and the circumstances under which our beliefs about it can be weakened or denied (see Weick, 1995 and/or Schwandt, 2002). In simpler terms, adoption of a vetted DQP by faculty leads necessarily to the issue of measurement of student learning. Whereas the consensus framework

Table 5.1. Types and Forms of Knowledge Representations Across Disciplinary Domains

Types of Knowledge Represented	Forms of Knowledge Representation		
	Propositional	Case-Based	Strategic
Subject Matter Content Knowledge	Principles Maxims Norms	Prototypes Precedents Parables	Contradictions Incompatibilities Conflicts
Applied Content Knowledge	Principles Maxims Norms	Prototypes Precedents Parables	Contradictions Incompatibilities Conflicts
Knowledge of Developmental Trajectory	Principles Maxims Norms	Prototypes Precedents Parables	Contradictions Incompatibilities Conflicts

identifies shared educational values, a theoretical framework that structures evaluation of students' demonstrations of learning emerges as necessary.

Thus, as we begin to use the DQP to probe expectations for student learning, the need for a coherent *theoretical* framework becomes readily apparent. We need a way of representing the specialized knowledge that grows in the minds of students as they develop pockets of domain-specific expertise. We are going to use Shulman's (1986) treatment of the development of knowledge for teaching as a template for a treatment of the development of specialized knowledge among aspiring associate degree graduates. Doing so acknowledges the need to differentiate different disciplines' distinct approaches to the development of general proficiencies while promoting consistency across the institution's curriculum. Offered here is a theoretical framework that derives from our experience working with the DQP.

Our theoretical framework distinguishes among three types of content knowledge: (a) subject matter content knowledge, (b) applied content knowledge, and (c) knowledge of developmental trajectory (Table 5.1).

Subject Matter Content Knowledge.   This category refers to the amount and organization of content knowledge in the mind of the student versus the expert. Although there are a number of ways to represent this content knowledge (Anderson & Krathwohl, 2001; Bloom et al., 1956; Gagné, 1965; Schwab, 1978), we are going to break with recent tradition and forsake Bloom and his revisionists in favor of Schwab. On Schwab's account, disciplines differ with regard to how expert knowledge is organized. Shulman (1986) summarizes as follows:

> For Schwab, the structures of a subject include both the substantive and the syntactic structures. The substantive structures are the variety of ways in which the basic concepts and principles of the discipline are organized to incorporate its facts. The syntactic structure of a discipline is the set of ways

in which the truth or falsehood, validity or invalidity, are established. When there exist competing claims regarding a given phenomenon, the syntax of a discipline provides the rules for determining which claim has greater warrant. A syntax is like a grammar. It is the set of rules for determining what is legitimate to say in a disciplinary domain and what "breaks" the rules. (p. 9)

Students may start with comprehension of facts and concepts but must eventually explain why accepted propositions are warranted, why this information is worth knowing, and how it relates to other propositions within and across disciplines, in theory and in practice.

Applied Content Knowledge.   This category of content knowledge goes beyond knowledge of subject matter *per se* to the dimension of subject matter knowledge for solving representative problems (or resolving representative dilemmas) within a domain of expertise. It is subject matter knowledge that is *reorganized for task performance in contexts relevant and appropriate to the discipline.*

Knowledge of Developmental Trajectory.   This category refers to knowledge of how novices develop into experts within disciplines or domains of expertise. It implies a progressive model of learning, in which knowledge accumulates gradually either through increased exposure to content or increased application of content.

Our framework also distinguishes three forms for representing each of the three types of content knowledge: (a) *propositional* knowledge, (b) *case* knowledge, and (c) *strategic* knowledge.

Propositional Knowledge.   Much of what is taught in the postsecondary classroom is still in the form of propositions, regardless of discipline. Some propositions are derived from research and application in practice; others, from the accumulated lore of experience. There are three types of propositional knowledge: *principles*, *maxims*, and *norms*. Each is derived from a different source of evidence.

1. *Principles.* Principles are derived from disciplined empirical or philosophical inquiry. These propositions make claims about the world that those in the discipline tend to agree are true, valid, legitimate, or otherwise warranted findings from empirical research or principled philosophical inquiry.
2. *Maxims.* Maxims are derived from practical experience. These propositions make practical rather than theoretical claims. In every field of study, there are unconfirmed beliefs, some of which are untestable. Nevertheless, these propositions represent the accumulated wisdom of disciplinary experts.
3. *Norms.* Norms are derived from moral or ethical reasoning. These propositions concern the disposition to act in accordance with a set of ideological or philosophical commitments that characterize the discipline. For instance, teachers are expected to uphold the values of

justice, fairness, and equity. These propositions guide the work of a teacher, not because they are empirically supported or because they work in practical terms, but because they represent the right thing to do.

Case knowledge. This form of knowledge representation involves specific, well-documented, richly described events. They may sound like narratives or anecdotes, but they are more than mere reports. Each case represents an instance of a larger class of events or incidents that can only be understood by invoking theoretical knowledge. It is not just a case, but *a case of something.*

Strategic Knowledge. This form of knowledge representation concerns those instances—theoretical, practical, and moral—in which one must deliberate about whether a claim is warranted or whether a course of action is appropriate for achieving practical or moral ends. In the history of every discipline and domain of expertise, there have been (or will be) instances in which theoretical principles contradict one another, in which recommendations for best practices are incompatible, in which ethical principles conflict. Strategic knowledge refers to the knowledge that must be invoked in order to adjudicate among claims and courses of action to resolve these dilemmas.

This theoretical framework better equips faculty to devise assignments that can be used to assess students' knowledge and learning of general proficiencies in ways that are distinct to particular disciplines and occupational-technical programs. The proficiencies in each area of the DQP describe complex combinations of skill and knowledge that are not attainable in a single learning experience or course. The various proficiencies and outcomes listed under each area imply competencies and outcomes that will, when taken together, lead students to the proficiencies described. But that poses a challenge for those trying to "tune" their own disciplinary courses (whether in general education programs or not), because multiple types of learning may be concealed by the breadth of the proficiency statements. Breaking out different forms of knowledge, as we have here, operationalizes the different types of learning the curricula help students attain. Faculty, as a result, are better able to think through the specific areas of knowledge and skill that comprise their disciplinary approaches to the proficiency areas in the DQP. It also supports the work of IR to provide tailored reports to different disciplines, understand better how to align and/or "roll-up" data on student learning from various levels across the institution, and can facilitate agreement on the aims and purposes of different portions of the curricula. The theoretical framework, therefore, provides an operational way for faculty to vet the DQP so that the proficiencies are broken down into assessable pieces of learning that can be incorporated into curricular and pedagogical practice. Our solution to the dilemma of measurement, however, opened a new dilemma, one of overall assessment.

NEW DIRECTIONS FOR INSTITUTIONAL RESEARCH • DOI: 10.1002/ir

A Practical Framework

To satisfy accreditors, colleges are required to conduct periodic evaluations of associate degree programs that include direct measures of student learning. Reynolds has a practical framework for program evaluation that resulted from principled empirical inquiry involving interviews, case studies, surveys, and observations of institutional work undertaken by program heads. This research program began in fall 2010 with the observation that annual reports of assessment activity rarely included the results of direct measures of student learning, and those that did seldom measured program-level learning outcomes in meaningful ways. Instead of reporting on their efforts to enhance student learning, program heads reported the results of their efforts to increase retention or graduation rates, build electronic advising platforms, complete training programs for online instruction, and assemble advisory panels. One might say we had a preexisting dilemma that needed attention.

Our work with the DQP, looking at the variety of program-level consensus frameworks and the various assessment strategies, resulted in a model for a comprehensive program evaluation composed of four integrated accounts or "master narratives" of program effectiveness. Most important here is the master narrative for the curriculum and instruction module. It is composed of three program-level goals: (a) ensuring external curriculum coherence, (b) ensuring internal curriculum coherence, and (c) documenting and enhancing student learning outcomes—and is prompted by a series of interviews or discussion questions that can help frame an assessment plan for a given program. These questions correspond to specific objectives, each of which corresponds to a measure (or set of measures) and a source (or sources) of evidence, and features a specific target for a given assessment cycle. If the target is not fully met, action plans address obstacles for the next assessment cycle.

As designed, each objective that has already been met remains active for the following cycle. This ensures that faculty created curriculum maps of where learning occurs and is assessed are reviewed and revised as necessary from year to year; that relevant audiences external to the program are kept apprised of changes and have the opportunity to confer with program heads about anticipated changes in bachelor's degree requirements and/or employer demands; that selected sites of program-level assessment remain appropriate and internally aligned, and so on. Centralizing the documentation of these efforts provides assurance to accreditors that these things are actually being done as they are being reported.

Goals and objectives are customized to associate degree programs of various types; but, it is still possible to aggregate findings across programs, in order to report out and establish institutional priorities for assessment. For instance, knowing how many occupational-technical programs were lacking a true capstone experience led to the funding proposal that made the course design workshop for capstone professors a reality. This was the forum in which the DQP was vetted with these program heads and other key faculty. Similarly, being able to characterize the lack of capstone experiences for students in college transfer programs as an obstacle to the institutional assessment plan (i.e., it is nearly impossible to locate near graduates of college transfer programs in specific courses) provides a policy lever for exploring the use of e-portfolio systems with students in college transfer programs and occupational-technical programs that cannot add capstones as standalone courses (for various reasons, including limits on the maximum number of hours required for the degree). This fact provided a rationale for including faculty seeking to design virtual capstones in the course design workshops, where they came face to face with the DQP.

Having in place a practical framework like the program review structure at Reynolds can help institutions prioritize their efforts to vet the DQP among those faculty who teach program-specific and general education coursework. Many institutions have already vetted the DQP while mapping program-level learning outcomes (step 1, involves faculty, faculty developers, program heads, assessment directors); but, these same programs may not have vetted their DQP-aligned, program-level consensus frameworks with professors at four-year institutions or with employers in the college's service area (step 2, involves program heads, key faculty, research analysts, advisory panels, local employers, key faculty at receiving institutions). When there is no capstone, or only a virtual capstone is feasible, there may be no single place where near graduates are being assessed on how well they integrate learning outcomes from across the curriculum in the types of academic or work contexts they will encounter in the near future.

The roles for data analysts—the traditional "institutional researchers" in community colleges—have typically been limited to mining a relational database to address external reporting requirements, administering and tabulating the results of perfunctory, one-size-fits-all surveys. In our work with the DQP, we discovered that IR's role can be expanded to the generation of information (e.g., triage reports) that program heads can use to make decisions about the curriculum design and the quality of instruction that program-declared students are receiving. The point here is that institutional research affecting the design, delivery, and assessment of associate level curricula and instruction must be approached as a *strategic enterprise*—one that is potentially enhanced by the introduction of the DQP at critical points in the assessment cycle.

Dilemmas and Lessons for IR

In our work with the DQP, four dilemmas emerged, modeled after those first invoked by Mark Windschitl (2002) to describe the types of challenges faced by K–12 teachers attempting to create constructivist

NEW DIRECTIONS FOR INSTITUTIONAL RESEARCH • DOI: 10.1002/ir

classrooms. Focusing upon the classroom teacher, Windschitl (1999, 2002) uses the term pedagogical instead of developmental. The latter term is used here so that it may apply to demands for expertise among all of those tasked with assembling arguments for student learning at the associate degree level. Those challenges, he reasoned, arise from difficulties conceptualizing constructivist theory, translating theory into practice, reenvisioning classroom culture, and encountering the politics of disrupting the *status quo* (i.e., the curriculum-centered, transmission model of instruction). Windschitl (1999) frames the constructivist agenda itself as the negotiation of these dilemmas. These challenges—conceptual, developmental, cultural, and political—arise for program heads, other teaching faculty, assessment directors, faculty developers, and policy makers at multiple levels of the organization. The quality agenda in higher education can also be viewed as the negotiation of these dilemmas, foregrounded against a national agenda to maximize access to higher education and enhance completion.

In our DQP project, it was our intent to support student success through designing a collaborative system to prevent loss and create momentum for aspiring and transferred students. In order to do so, we had to identify the loss points, implement momentum strategies, and set and interpret success metrics appropriate for each stage of student progression. As part of our work we thus explored nine different moments of transfer success including connection, entry, progression, completion at Reynolds—but also connection, entry point 1, entry point 2, progress, and completion at VCU. For each of the nine instances of transfer success we explored possible loss points and momentum strategies that could serve as interventions. Although that may sound like a rather reasonable and straightforward process, when assessing learning and determining the success points as part of the DQP work, the four conceptual dilemmas mentioned above required project navigation.

When IR is attempting to define transfer success, we need to be aware of the policy environment and conceptual issues therein. For instance, what is transfer success and what makes a strong argument for transfer success? What evidence can be used to tell a coherent, evidence-centered story about transfer? Does it include elements of student access? Educational quality? And how does the DQP work fit in? Without a wider lens to the role of IR in institutional quality discussions, it is easy to provide reports or pull data without ensuring—especially when engaging with a partner institution— that *conceptually* the teams are discussing, in agreement, and using the same concepts (in this instance as it relates to transfer).

Developmentally, as the project matured and moved through its various stages we had to repeatedly ask: Do we have the knowledge, skills, and dispositions necessary for the task? Are faculty able to develop assignments in alignment with the DQP and is leadership aware and supportive of the work? Are IR and assessment staff able to represent student learning in a means that moves beyond reporting or anecdote? Each of these questions was related to and informed by the conceptual dilemmas mentioned before and influenced the creation of the workshops and requests for administrative support needed to further the DQP project. Yet at any point in time, if the project did not align culturally, all may have been for naught. Examination of cultural dilemmas includes awareness of the roles, beliefs, norms, and practices that are shared versus unshared by organizations and those within. When working in partnership with the transfer institution, exploration of such norms is vital such that implicit working routines are made transparent to partner institutions to advance the ability of the institutions to work in partnership with each other toward shared ends.

Finally, political dilemmas abound in this work, as evidenced by the discussion of the issues with viewing the DQP as a normative framework in prior sections of this chapter. DQP and Tuning work necessarily require large-scale cross-campus engagement of faculty, staff, students, administrators, and others—groups that may not be used to working collectively on projects. Thus political dilemmas include exploration of what might promote collaboration versus competition amongst partner institutions and their requisite personnel. It is useful for project teams to explore how the relationships among faculty, students, administrators, and others might be disrupted when engaging in discussion of the meaning of a degree and issues of transfer.

Institutional researchers can serve as useful navigators for others involved in the project by leading discussions to reach shared meaning on various measures and metrics of interest. Further, evidence can be provided in various formats to different audiences within the teams to support their internal dialogue and discussion. Yet, before undertaking large-scale knowledge construction of this kind across campus, this article has made the argument that a necessary first step is exploration of the frameworks that will guide the work along with the processes that will support the frameworks and those on the ground engaging with students.

References

Anderson, L., & Krathwohl, D. A. (2001). *Taxonomy for learning, teaching and assessing: A revision of Bloom's Taxonomy of Educational Objectives*. New York: Longman.

Berg, J., Grimm, L. M., Wigmore, D., Cratsley, C. K., Slotnick, R. C., & Taylor, S. (2014). Quality collaborative to assess quantitative reasoning: Adapting the LEAP VALUE rubric and the DQP. *Peer Review, 16*(3), 17–23.

Bloom, B. S. (Ed.), Engelhart, M. D., Furst, E. J., Hill, W. H., & Krathwohl, D. R. (1956). *Taxonomy of educational objectives: The classification of educational goals. Handbook 1: Cognitive domain*. New York, NY: David McKay.

Gagné, R. M. (1965). *The condition of learning*. New York: Holt, Rinehart and Winston.

Jankowski, N. A., & Marshall, D. W. (2014). *Roadmap to enhanced student learning: Implementing the DQP and Tuning*. Urbana, IL: National Institute for Learning Outcomes Assessment and Institute for Evidence-Based Change.

Lumina Foundation for Education. (2011). *The Degree Qualifications Profile*. Indianapolis, IN: Author.

Schwab, J. J. (1978). The practical: A language for curriculum. In I. Westbury & N. J. Wilkof (Eds.), *Science, curriculum, and liberal education: Selected essays* (pp. 287–321). Chicago, IL: University of Chicago Press.

Schwandt, T. A. (2002). *Evaluation practice reconsidered.* New York, NY: Peter Lang Publishing.

Shulman, L. S. (1986). Those who understand: Knowledge growth in teaching. *Educational Research, 15*(4), 4–14.

Weick, K. E. (1995). *Sensemaking in organizations.* Thousand Oaks, CA: Sage.

Windschitl, M. (1999). The challenges of sustaining a constructivist classroom culture. *Phi Delta Kappan, 80,* 751–757.

Windschitl, M. (2002). Framing constructivism in practice as the negotiation of dilemmas: An analysis of the conceptual, pedagogical, cultural and political challenges facing teachers. *Review of Educational Research, 72,* 131–175.

SANDRA FULTON BATH *is an assessment and institutional research consultant with J. Sargeant Reynolds Community College in Richmond, VA, and former coordinator of assessment and institutional research with Reynolds.*

NEW DIRECTIONS FOR INSTITUTIONAL RESEARCH • DOI: 10.1002/ir

6

This concluding essay provides a glimpse to the future and alerts IR professionals to related initiatives as well as provides an update to ongoing work with DQP and Tuning. Pulling from the prior chapters it provides some implications for IR offices to consider, not only in their work with the DQP and Tuning, but in terms of general decision support.

New Directions for IR, the DQP, and Tuning

Natasha A. Jankowski, David W. Marshall

The preceding essays by Jessica Ickes and Daniel Flowers, Robert Sweatman, and Sandi Fulton Bath each describe activities and procedures undertaken in early work with the Degree Qualifications Profile (DQP) that used the so-called "beta version" released in 2011 for testing by institutions of higher education. In October 2014, Lumina Foundation released a revised DQP after its four authors, Clifford Adelman, Peter Ewell, Paul Gaston, and Carol Geary Schneider, reviewed work with the beta version and responses to its contents. As a result, the DQP now reflects thoughtful input from scores of individuals and organizations that have reviewed and worked with the DQP in its original form. The DQP now represents a large, collaborative effort to define the meaning of degrees in terms of scaffolded learning.

This result suggests that work with the Degree Qualifications Profile has spawned what might be considered a national dialogue around the meaning of degrees but not a dialogue detached from pragmatic application of the conversations. With the DQP as a centerpiece, individuals, institutions of higher education, and associations and organizations working in and on higher education have engaged in an examination of what U.S. higher education strives to help students achieve. Although institutions make very different uses of the DQP and turn to it to deal with differing concerns, a core definition of American higher learning has emerged as an important national discussion, a discussion that includes not just the kind of feedback received by the DQP's authors but also journals such as this one, conference presentations, and the recently launched *Tuning Journal for Higher Education.*

Despite its revision, fundamentally the DQP remains much as it was in 2011, organized around the five proficiency areas described earlier in

NEW DIRECTIONS FOR INSTITUTIONAL RESEARCH, no. 165 © 2015 Wiley Periodicals, Inc.
Published online in Wiley Online Library (wileyonlinelibrary.com) • DOI: 10.1002/ir.20125

this issue, and the substance of the proficiencies are not significantly changed, though there are revisions that respond to the advice and experience of those providing feedback to the DQP's authors and the National Institute for Learning Outcomes Assessment. To address that feedback, the authors created new proficiency statements concerning ethical reasoning and put greater emphasis on global learning while strengthening statements on quantitative reasoning. The authors of the DQP also increased emphasis on three key areas: independent investigation at all degree levels; field-transcendent analytical, cooperative approaches to learning; and integration of intellectual skills with broad, specialized, applied, and civic learning.

The DQP now also includes greater support for those individuals and institutions using it. After requests for resources related to assessment, the authors identified resources that support the assessment of DQP proficiencies. A preliminary lexicon that offers definitions for higher education terms as used in the DQP was added, too, as well as clarification of the resemblances or commonalities between the DQP and the Tuning process. This last topic deserves greater attention here, because several projects have been launched that brought both the proficiencies in the DQP and the process of Tuning together since the release of the DQP's beta version.

DQP and Tuning Together

Since 2012, three projects in particular, those organized by the American Historical Association (AHA), the National Communication Association (NCA), and the Accrediting Commission for Community and Junior Colleges (ACCJC), engaged with both tools. Even though each project's leaders turned to the DQP and Tuning for different, though similar, reasons, there emerged clear patterns of benefit in using the DQP with Tuning's approaches to defining learning in two distinct areas: improved procedures for working with the DQP and increased sensitivity to integrative learning.

Procedures for Working with DQP. In projects that have taken the DQP as their starting point, there has often been some uncertainty about a proper way to proceed from what can be an overwhelming, if not stimulating description of student learning. This challenge emerged rather dramatically in the National Communication Association's quasi-experimental initiative. NCA convened a faculty work group of 30 members, who were divided into three teams. Each team approached work with the DQP and Tuning from a different starting point. The first began by generating outcomes that define the discipline's essential learning before mapping them to the DQP, the second began by examining the DQP before defining essential learning in communication, and the third consulted the DQP and used it as a framework for defining disciplinary-specific learning outcomes. The group to start with the DQP struggled at the outset, with some

New Directions for Institutional Research • DOI: 10.1002/ir

members indicating that the static nature of the DQP, with its lists of proficiency statements, demands a response, but does not point to a particular way of responding. Because the DQP provides descriptions of learning without prescribing a way of working with those descriptions, members of this group felt uncertain as to how to proceed. In contrast, the group that worked simultaneously with both the DQP and the Tuning process found that the DQP provided a framework in which they could begin to describe discipline-specific knowledge. For them, the DQP provided a structuring device for organizing their discussions of learning in the discipline of communication.

Some institutions that have taken up the DQP have found a similar conundrum, and have found Tuning to be the means of working productively with the DQP. In ACCJC's DQP initiative, several colleges have, in effect, "tuned" disciplines to the DQP. For example, West Hills College Coalinga worked on aligning degree-level learning outcomes to the DQP's proficiency areas, choosing to focus on two disciplines, agriculture technology science and administration of justice, both in career-technical education programs. Shasta College undertook a very similar approach, working with the departments of communication and mathematics. In each case, faculty in disciplines effectively "tuned" their outcomes, reconsidering them and aligning them with the DQP. Tuning in this context differs from the large, national projects such as NCA's in that a single institution and a single department is defining or refining learning outcomes, but fundamentally the process is the same. For projects such as those at West Hills and Shasta, faculty used the DQP as a structuring framework within which they revised their outcomes to align with the proficiencies described in the DQP. Those programs did so not in a disciplinary vacuum but in dialogue with both the DQP and other personnel on their campuses. Tuning, thus, becomes an approach to engaging with the DQP. Although Tuning has traditionally been an endeavor that draws faculty from disparate institutions together to define learning in a discipline, Tuning's flexible methodology of outcomes development and consultation has provided discipline faculty in individual institutions a process to work more productively with the DQP. Coupling Tuning processes in consideration of the DQP has, moreover, resulted in a deeper consideration of how discipline-specific study and general proficiencies relate within the curricula and pedagogies of particular programs.

Sensitivity to Integrative Learning and Its Ramifications.   In line with the DQP authors' emphasis on the integration of learning, the projects that engaged both DQP and Tuning found that there was an increased understanding of and sensitivity to integrative learning. This understanding takes three different, but closely related forms: Inclusion of general proficiencies in specialized programs; consideration of disciplinary contributions to general education, and; a clearer definition of relationships between educational segments.

Inclusion of General Proficiencies.   In early Tuning projects, which were nearly all state based and drawing on institutions from around the given state, discipline-specific faculty groups wrestled with how to deal with general competencies. Their discussions were often focused and fruitful when they worked to define the essence of the discipline in the form of learning outcomes, but that step away from specialized knowledge (to use the language of the DQP) to general skills and knowledge often resulted in underdeveloped thinking. Projects tended to pull generic lists from books on the subject and allow them to sit alongside, but not integrated into, the emergent definition of the discipline's essential learning.

Because the DQP offers proficiencies that are threaded together with common competencies, when Tuning projects introduced the DQP into discussions, faculty work groups began to conceptualize their own disciplinary curricula and pedagogies as not just reinforcing general proficiencies typically relegated to general education but even depending on them. For the National Communication Association, for example, faculty participants developed their learning outcomes in Communication in reference to the DQP. Their outcomes, interestingly, mirror the integrative, threaded structure of the DQP, with different outcomes explicitly referencing different areas of the DQP and referencing other parts of the learning outcomes in communication. As a result, the emergent image of education in the discipline is one that is attuned to how competencies associated with general education programs are addressed in courses within the major.

Although, no doubt, faculty across the country are aware of the need to attend to general competencies and proficiencies, general education (GE) is largely relegated to the first 2 years of a student's education, after which study of the "more important" subject matter of the major is undertaken—often with an assumption that general education has "trained" students for that work. The shift that combined use of DQP and Tuning has encouraged now reimagines that dichotomous image of higher education. Within these projects, learning begins to be perceived as more recursive and iterative, with faculty more clearly identifying their own roles in reinforcing the knowledge and skills learned in general education. The increased understanding of an iterative approach to learning is an actionable takeaway for faculty participants in these projects. Pedagogies and assignments can be more intentionally constructed to promote student learning in the major while applying knowledge and skills from other domains. This is precisely where programs will find the necessity of institutional research (IR). If learning is perceived and promoted as spanning across the curriculum and is, as a result, developed in multiple departments—or even cocurricula—then faculty and staff can no longer work on siloed assessment of student learning and program effectiveness. Their data needs will encompass a wider view of learning. They may need combined reports on data about how students move through the curriculum as a whole. They may need reports that reveal how students perform in general education or even how students perform in GE in comparison to majors or field-specific programs.

Disciplinary Contributions to General Education.   The increased awareness of the ways in which general proficiencies can be incorporated into discipline-specific learning has brought with it a reflexive move in these projects. Faculty participating in these initiatives have begun to identify the distinct ways in which their disciplines contribute to learning in general education programs. If study in a major contributes simultaneously to development of general proficiencies, then faculty have asked what distinctive contribution disciplines stand to make in general education. Just as courses in, say, history can reinforce those proficiencies, historians began asking what unique approach to knowledge and learning their discipline offers to students. Discussions have turned toward what might be called "differential epistemologies" with consideration of the threshold concepts that define disciplinary approaches.

Working toward this perspective has resulted in interest in rethinking courses for nonmajors. For example, the American Historical Association has begun to conceive of specific disciplines and DQP as existing in an orthogonal relationship, with their point of intersection being actualized in general education courses such as the introductory history classes required of students around the country. AHA has considered launching a project to use Tuning as a methodology for defining the learning (and learning outcomes) that could ideally structure such courses so that they attend to general proficiencies while adding disciplinarily knowledge and skills. As of this writing, that project has not yet been undertaken.

Defining Relationships Between Educational Segments.   This turn to thinking about the iterative and recursive nature of learning in relation to general education and a major field of study has concomitantly affected how 2-year and 4-year faculty conceptualize the relationship between community colleges and baccalaureate institutions. Conversations of transfer and articulation have taken a step back from the simplistic pragmatics of course descriptions toward more nuanced discussions of scaffolded outcomes that define levels of learning appropriate to what might be called "benchmark moments," such as the end of 2 years of study, the end of 4 years of study, and the completion of a master's degree. By defining outcomes attentive to general proficiencies and to knowledge and skills in the major, faculty on these projects have begun to redefine the tasks of educators around a progressive description of student learning that seems to give all faculty a shared stake in both areas of learning.

This is a somewhat radical (even if only nascent) shift away from arguments about "mission creep" and the muddied articulation of learning as students transfer among institutions. This shift also has interesting implications for IR, because it implies an analysis of student learning that is progressive and potentially split across multiple campuses. Data needs may shift toward understanding the extent to which transfer and native student populations fare differently in academic programs and how, and toward identifying how native and transfer students' performance of general proficiencies compares. If Tuning projects such as AHA's and NCA's have encouraged discussions of learning across educational segments, then the implication may mean offices of institutional research need to work in a similarly collaborative way across segments.

Related Initiatives and Available Resources

For IR professionals interested in working with the DQP and Tuning, there are a variety of resources available to support such efforts. In addition, work with the DQP has connected to other initiatives, bringing different areas of effort together around making sense of degree-level proficiencies. This section provides a brief introduction to related initiatives in which IR may have an interest as well as presents resources to advance institutional engagement with DQP and Tuning.

DQP and Tuning Resources. For IR professionals interested in learning more about institutional work with the DQP and Tuning or to investigate other institutions doing this work, the DQP/Tuning website is a valuable resource (http://degreeprofile.org). Regularly updated information housed on the site includes a resource kit, access to copies of the DQP, institutional examples and the option to join an email list for updates. In addition, institutions have the opportunity to request a DQP/Tuning coach. Coaches are from institutions who have worked with the DQP or Tuning, are experienced in assessment and assignment design, and represent a variety of institutional types and backgrounds from faculty, administration, and related staff. They are available for a free 1-day visit to a campus to facilitate workshops and assist in implementation efforts. Coaches are matched to institutions based on the needs of the campus and the trajectory of the work. Further, for institutions working with the DQP, we invite you to complete an institutional activity report, available on the website, which provides information about work with the DQP from which others can learn.

Finally, IR practitioners may be interested in the DQP Assignment Library that houses peer-reviewed faculty designed assignments that are aligned to proficiencies outlined in the DQP. Informational resources are available for those interested in conducting assignment design workshops on their own campus or for submitting assignments to the library through an online peer review process (http://assignmentlibrary.org). Additional available resources related to assessment can be found on the National Institute for Learning Outcomes Assessment (NILOA) website (http://learningoutcomesassessment.org).

Related Initiatives. Conversations on the meaning and quality of degrees based upon student learning as opposed to seat time have connected to various strands of work. Three strands are worth mentioning here including work addressing assessing student learning, efforts around defining credentials, and resource hubs.

Assessment.   For the assessment of student learning, much of the work with DQP has included utilization of the Association of American Colleges and Universities (AAC&U) VALUE rubrics or alignment with prior-learning assessments. The AAC&U VALUE rubrics were designed by teams of faculty and educational professionals from across U.S. higher education (http://aacu.org/value/rubrics). There are 16 rubrics, each includes a cover sheet of definitions and a second page encompassing the rubric itself. Faculty at over 100 college campuses tested drafts of the rubrics. The rubrics are available for download from the AAC&U website along with additional information about norming and their use. Since the release of the rubrics in 2010 they have been viewed at more than 5,600 discrete institutions (including schools and associations) and more than 3,300 colleges and universities in the United States and around the world.

A project referred to as the Multi-State Collaborative (MSC) has used the VALUE rubrics to provide evidence about student achievement of learning outcomes from across nine states (http://www.sheeo.org/projects /msc-multi-state-collaborative-advance-learning-outcomes-assessment). It is an attempt to move from standardized testing to producing reports around actual student work through use of common rubrics. The MSC is designed to produce valid data summarizing faculty judgments of students' own work, and also seeks to aggregate results that allows for benchmarking across institutions and states. The project is led by the State Higher Education Executive Officers Association (SHEEO) and AAC&U.

The Council for Adult and Experiential Learning (CAEL) supports efforts around prior-learning assessment, a process for students to earn college credit for learning acquired from work experience, training, military, or other means. Their efforts to align the workforce and education in ways that value prior learning have produced useful research on workforce education, programs that have turned to competency-based learning, and demographic challenges to the success of such initiatives.

Credentials.   Regarding defining credentials, two efforts including the development of a credentialing registry and the national dialogue around connecting credentials are worth mentioning. George Washington University and two partner organizations are in the process of building and testing a credential registry (http://credentialtransparencyinitiative.org/). The purpose of the registry is to allow users, including employers, students, and institutions, to compare various information on a variety of workforce credentials encompassing college degrees and industry certifications. The growth of credentials including certificates, licenses, and microcredentials such as badges has led to confusion regarding the quality, value, and comparability of credentials. The project brings together employers, higher education organizations, and institutions to discuss the registry development and necessary metrics and related information. Information that populates the registry will come from institutional websites.

Connecting Credentials is a project calling for ways to better align the diverse and fragmented credentialing system into a learning-based and student-centered framework (http://connectingcredentials.org/). The project is currently inviting institutions and organizations to join in a national dialogue to ensure educational quality and increased understanding of the various credentials available to students. In fall 2015 a national summit will take place including more than 100 organizations to create a plan for achieving changes in credentialing policy and practice as well as begin a broader public dialogue around credentials. Coupled to this work has been the start of a project led by registrars and student affairs professionals to develop alternative transcripts documenting student learning from across the curricula and cocurricula.

Resources.   For resource hubs of use to IR two efforts are presented here, the Competency-Based Education Network and the efforts of the AAC&U Faculty Collaboratives. The Competency-Based Education Network (http://www.cbenetwork.org) is composed of a group of 30 colleges and universities with 82 campuses working together to address shared challenges to designing, developing and scaling competency-based degree programs. Participating institutions take part in research efforts to advance high-quality competency-based education programs. Member institutions either currently offer competency-based degree programs or are on their way to creating them. For those not familiar, competency-based education programs provide a flexible means for students to acquire credit for what they know and can do and to build on their knowledge by moving through learning at their own pace. Students in competency-based education programs demonstrate their knowledge and skills through multiple forms of assessment and many of the projects are designed to be flexible options for students not well served by existing postsecondary programs. Participating students receive necessary support through intensive guidance and faculty and staff support and are able to accelerate their time to degree to save additional time and costs.

The work of the AAC&U Faculty Collaboratives project focused upon connecting a variety of efforts to help faculty leaders make sense of and participate in student success initiatives (http://www.aacu.org/faculty). The goal of the Faculty Collaboratives is to create a wide-reaching, sustainable network of resources and innovation hubs for faculty learning. The work is occurring in 10 states focused upon diffusing knowledge and practice through community collections of faculty. The network is specifically tasked with providing support to the DQP and Tuning as well as other initiatives. The goal of the collaboratives is to build capacity related to work with DQP and Tuning for general education and improved student persistence and learning. Finally, the project seeks to document "what works" as explored through scholarship of teaching and learning projects.

NEW DIRECTIONS FOR INSTITUTIONAL RESEARCH • DOI: 10.1002/ir

Final Thoughts

This issue of *New Directions for Institutional Research* offered an explanation of the DQP and Tuning that foregrounds the potential impact of these initiatives on IR. The increased attention to the meaning of U.S. degrees and the DQP's new strengthening of integrative, field-transcending work has implications for offices of institutional research. This is all the more true as institutions begin to think more fully about strategies for gathering data on student and program performance in curricula, cocurricula, and pedagogies that attempt to actualize the kinds of proficiencies described in the DQP and developed by Tuning initiatives. In other words, as institutions and their faculty and staff begin to move toward decision making reinforced by data about patterns of strengths and weaknesses in student learning, they will need new forms of support from IR.

This pronouncement is likely not an earth-shattering one for institutional researchers. After all, the Association of Institutional Research (AIR) has recently offered its "Brief Summary of Statements of Aspirational Practice for Institutional Research" for feedback (based on which it is revising those statements), as mentioned in the chapter by Jankowski and Kinzie. The two-page document describes not a profound paradigm shift but a revision of focus for institutional researchers, one marked by an emphasis on the use of data to strengthen student success in institutions of higher education. AIR's "Statements" point to the increase in data use by offices and personnel who have not traditionally been associated with its use and a resulting need to shift IR activities toward actionable data and data use to make change, rather than the presentation of data. A key aspect of this need, according to the "Statements," is the provision of department- and program-specific data with tools for accessing it more easily.

In part, we are describing a more active involvement by IR in the decision support of the assessment of student learning outcomes by faculty and staff. Traditionally, faculty and staff have developed their own processes for outcomes assessment whereas IR provided administrators with data concerning larger student and institution performance trends. As institutions using the DQP and Tuning begin to turn toward more integrative programs of learning, however, there are only rarely assessment offices prepared to facilitate the kinds of field-transcending learning that those institutions are attempting to establish. Offices of institutional research may be better equipped to help generate the kinds of actionable data about patterns in student learning that meaningful outcomes assessment depends on. For example, as departments restructure curricula around progressive models of learning or as they evaluate the need to do so, IR offices may need to provide data about course taking patterns that help faculty identify where curricular structures facilitate or inhibit learning. Such data will enable faculty to work from a data-informed position as they make changes to curricula and pedagogies.

Playing that role, however, will likely require institutional researchers to take part in committees and early planning discussions for the construction of assessment systems that are capable of providing useful information about the patterns of student behavior and performance that can enable faculty and staff to take action toward impactful change. Such involvement may not occur to faculty and staff, who are accustomed to working from very different models of assessment, but therein lies the fundamental role for IR: being experts in the production of data and highly skilled in the interpretation of it makes an office of institutional research an essential component to discussion of student success that cuts across disciplinary and even institutional lines. Early involvement in discussions prepares faculty and staff to begin learning from IR about what kinds of actionable data can be produced and how. Conversely, institutional researchers need to become aware of what kinds of data faculty and staff find most useful. Both sides of this relationship can learn from one another to begin constructing new forms of data collection, analysis, and presentation that will enable institutions to be strategically responsive to program and student needs.

Part of the challenge here is the emerging need to produce and provide data to disparate programs that have never had to collaborate on outcomes assessment in the ways necessitated by use of the DQP and Tuning. If, as we have described, institutions begin threading general proficiencies throughout both general education and majors more intentionally than in previous years, and if institutions revise curricula and pedagogies to better reflect the cross-cutting knowledge and skills that tools like DQP and Tuning provide, then institutions will require an information hub capable of coordinating data collection across those disparate units. A concomitant challenge for institutional research will be a need to divide IR's focus from the kinds of "pure" research activities that have dominated offices to include "applied research" activities of widespread, authentic assessment across the institution. One can easily understand, then, that data presentation and visualization will become increasingly important, particularly for programs not accustomed to such work.

The contributors to this issue have offered varying pictures of what these roles may look like. Ickes and Flowers supported campus efforts by providing survey data from multiple stakeholder groups that revealed the need for conversations to be cross-cutting so that the campus could reach consensus on outcomes. Sweatman coordinated and led the efforts around rubric development and use. His work enabled a coupling of assessment and faculty engagement with an eye toward strong methodologies and proper rubric use. And Sandra Fulton Bath points to the dilemmas that will be raised by this work and how IR may need to traverse them to provide the type of decision support described in this chapter. For instance, she points to the need to account for the roles, beliefs, norms, and practices that may be shared or not between institutions in efforts to gather data around matters of student transfer and success. The chapters written by IR practitioners

NEW DIRECTIONS FOR INSTITUTIONAL RESEARCH • DOI: 10.1002/ir

indicate that the shifts described above are occurring, and IR is well positioned to address them. Although the amount of refocusing or reorientation of IR is connected to the particular needs of an institution, the larger movement of the field to become an active part of change conversations across the campus setting is well underway.

Natasha A. Jankowski is associate director of the National Institute for Learning Outcomes Assessment and research assistant professor in the department of Education Policy, Organization and Leadership at the University of Illinois Urbana-Champaign.

David W. Marshall is associate professor of English at California State University San Bernardino and serves as director of Tuning USA with the Institute for Evidence-Based Change.

Index

Abedi, J., 49

Abrams, R., 51

ACCJC. *See* Accrediting Commission for Community and Junior Colleges (ACCJC)

Accrediting Commission for Community and Junior Colleges (ACCJC), 8, 78, 83, 84

Adam, A. J., 16

Adelman, C., 3, 7, 8, 77

Algina, J., 51

Alig, J. L., 16

Alvarez, C. A., 51

Anderson, L., 69

Ariovich, L., 23

Arter, J., 48–50

Baartman, L. K. J., 45

Baker, E. L., 49

Barlow, J., 57

Bastiaens, T. J., 45

Bath, S. F., 61, 76, 77

Behrens, J. T., 48

Beneitone, P., 5

Berg, J., 64

Bers, T. H., 15–17

Blaszczyk, A. T., 51

Bloom, B. S., 69

Bresciani, M. J., 57

Brittingham, B., 16

CAEL. *See* Council for Adult and Experiential Learning (CAEL)

Calderon, A., 16, 17

Canaday, D., 51

Chappuis, J., 48–50

Competency-Based Education Network, 84

Consensus framework, DQP and, 62–66; relationship to Tuning, 65–66; student proficiencies, 62

Council for Adult and Experiential Learning (CAEL), 83

Cratsley, C. K., 64

Crocker, L., 51

Crosson, P., 23

Daniel, C., 48

Degree Qualifications Profile (DQP), 7–9; assessment process, plan for coordinating, 44–56. *See also* DQP assessment; core areas under, 7; feedback from, 9; information on work of, 11–12; learning outcomes, gap analysis, 28–34; outcomes, student feedback on, 34–37; overview, 3–4; in practice, 61–75; procedures for working with, 78–79; related initiatives, 82–84; revised, 39–40; testing, 27–40; Tuning and, 6, 9–11, 78–82; and Tuning resources, 82; WASC guidelines, 8

Delandshere, G., 47

Delaney, A. M., 16

Dellinger, A., 48

Denner, P. R., 48

Denny, R. K., 48

DeRemer, M. L., 48

Dilemmas Facing IR in Community Colleges, framework of, 61–75; consensus framework, 62–66; normative framework, 66–68; practical framework, 72–73; theoretical framework, 68–71

Dilemmas facing IR in community colleges, framework of, 73–75

DQP. *See* Degree Qualifications Profile (DQP)

DQP assessment: action on results of, 55–56; application of rubrics to measure student proficiency, 49; credible validity argument, building of, 52–54; internal consistency reliability, establishment of, 51–52; investigation of reliability and validity, 50–54; performance related to outcomes, rubric development, 46–49; program faculty member, model for, 45; rubric norming, 49–50; rubric ratings for evidence of student learning, analysis of, 54; summarization of results of, 54–55

DQP Assignment Library, 82
Duncan, K., 57

Engelhart, M. D., 69
Ewell, P. T., 7, 8, 10, 13, 21, 77

Fike, D. S., 51
Fincher, C. L., 16
Flowers, D. R., 1, 22, 27, 35, 40, 41, 77
Frisbie, D. A., 51
Fulton, S., 23
Furst, E. J., 69

Gagné, R. M., 69
Gasper, E., 51
Gaston, P. L., 3, 7, 8, 77
Gonzalez, J., 5
Gordon, B., 48
Grimm, L. M., 64

Harris, L. B., 48
Hill, W. H., 69
Holloway, A., 27
Holmes, C., 49, 50
Howard, R. D., 37
Hutchings, P., 8, 13, 21

Ickes, J. L., 1, 22, 27, 35, 40, 41, 77
IEBC. See Institute for Evidence-Based
    Change (IEBC)
Ikenberry, S. O., 16, 23
Institute for Evidence-Based Change
    (IEBC), 61
Institutional research, roles of, 15–25;
    bcome part of conversation, 22; col-
    laboration and coordination, 23; as
    data support, 18–19; in DQP/Tuning
    efforts, 20–22; as evidence support,
    20; facilitating alignment, 23; as fac-
    ulty support, 19–20; focus areas of,
    16; institutional examples, 17–20; as
    leader, 18; organizing data for decision
    making, 23; as partner, 18; and trans-
    fer, 20
Integrative learning, sensitivity and ram-
    ifications of, 79–82; disciplinary con-
    tributions to general education, 81;
    general proficiencies, inclusion of,
    80–81; relationships between educa-
    tional segments, 81–82

Jankowski, N. A., 1–3, 6, 8, 10, 11, 13,
    15, 16, 21, 23, 26, 77, 87
Johnson, E., 48
Johnson, R. L., 48
Jonsson, A., 47, 48, 50, 51

Kahn, A., 48
Kelly, H. A., 17
Kinzie, J., 1, 13, 15, 16, 23, 26
Kirschner, P. A., 45
Knight, W. E., 37
Koency, G., 48
Kolkhorst, F., 57
Konheim-Kalkstein, Y. L., 47, 51
Krathwohl, D. A., 69
Krathwohl, D. R., 69
Kuh, D., 13
Kuh, G. D., 16, 23

LEAP. See Liberal Education America's
    Promise (LEAP)
Leydens, J., 47, 52, 53
Liberal Education America's Promise
    (LEAP), 7
Linn, R. L., 49
Lumina Foundation, 3, 4, 6

MacLaughlin, E. J., 51
Maki, P. L., 50, 55
Manor, J. E., 47, 51
Marshall, D. W., 2, 3, 6, 8, 11, 13, 77, 87
Marzano, R. J., 48, 49
Massey, A. R., 47, 51
Mathies, C., 16, 17
Matier, M. W., 16
McLaughlin, G. W., 37
Michaels, M., 48
Middaugh, M. F., 17
Moskal, B. M., 47, 52, 53
Myford, C. M., 48

National Institute for Learning Out-
    comes Assessment (NILOA), 11, 17–
    18, 21, 23, 82
Nebeker, C., 57
Niemi, D., 49
NILOA. See National Institute for Learn-
    ing Outcomes Assessment (NILOA)
Normative framework, DQP and, 66–68;
    changed human beings, 67; human
    change agents, 68; Tuning efforts, 67

Oakleaf, M., 49, 50, 57
O'Brien, P. M., 16
Orcutt, B., 23

Penny, J., 48
Persky, H., 48
Petrosky, A., 47
Popp, S. E. O., 48
Powers, T., 48
Priddy, L., 27

Rafilson, F., 53
Reynolds-Sundet, R., 16
Richman, W. A., 23
Rink, J., 49
Rogers, G., 27
Rowley, G. L., 51
Ryan, J. M., 48

SACS. See Schools Commission on
    Colleges (SACS)
Salzman, S. A., 48
Saupe, J. L., 16
Schmidtlein, F. A., 17
Schmitz, J. A. P., 47, 51
Schneider, C. G., 8, 77
Schools Commission on Colleges
    (SACS), 8
Schwab, J. J., 69
Schwandt, T. A., 68
Seifert, C. F., 51
SHEEO. See State Higher Education Ex-
    ecutive Officers Association (SHEEO)
Shulman, L. S., 69
Sidle, C. C., 16
Slotnick, R. C., 64
State Higher Education Executive Offi-
    cers Association (SHEEO), 83
Stellmack, M. A., 47, 51
Stemler, S. E., 51
Stoddart, T., 51
Stuhlmann, J., 48
Suskie, L., 38
Svingby, G., 47, 48, 50, 51
Sweatman, R. A., 1, 23, 43, 59, 77

Taylor, S., 64
Terenzini, P., 16
Theoretical framework, DQP, 68–71; ap-
    plied content knowledge, 70; case
    knowledge, 71; knowledge of de-
    velopmental trajectory, 70; proposi-
    tional knowledge, 70–71; strategic
    knowledge, 71; subject matter content
    knowledge, 69–70
Thompson, M. S., 48
Traub, R. E., 51
Tuning: consensus building and qual-
    ity assurance by, 6–7; definition of,
    4; disciplines and states sponsor, 5;
    DQP projects and, 6, 9–11; fundamen-
    tal values of, 6; goals and principles
    of, 11; information on work of, 11–12;
    initiatives, 4–5; overview, 3–4
Tuning Journal for Higher Education, 77

Van der Vleuten, C. P. M., 45
VCU. See Virginia Commonwealth
    University (VCU)
Virginia Commonwealth University
    (VCU), 63–64
Volkwein, F., 15, 17, 23
Voorhees, R. A., 16

Wagenaar, R., 5
Walters, A. M., 17
Waltman, K., 48
WASC. See Western Association of
    Schools and Colleges (WASC)
Wehlburg, C., 16
Weick, K. E., 68
Weigle, S. C., 48
Western Association of Schools and Col-
    leges (WASC), 8
Wigmore, D., 64
Wilkins, R., 48
Williams, L., 49
Windschitl, M., 73, 74
Woodley, A., 16

Zimmaro, D. M., 47

OTHER TITLES AVAILABLE IN THE
NEW DIRECTIONS FOR INSTITUTIONAL RESEARCH SERIES
John F. Ryan, Editor-in-Chief
Gloria Crisp, Associate Editor

IR 164   **Measuring Cocurricular Learning: The Role of the IR Office**
Lance C. Kennedy-Phillips, Angela Baldasare, Michael N. Christakis
Scholars and practitioners agree that learning takes place both inside and
outside of the classroom. This volume of *New Directions for Institutional
Research* examines the complexities of measuring co-curricular learning and
discusses the role of the institutional research professional in measuring
learning outside of the classroom. Institutional research professionals are
often called upon to demonstrate achievement of university goals and
priorities. The out of classroom, or co-curricular, experience in some form is
usually a part of those goals. This volume will explore:
• contemporary theories around co-curricular learning and its influence on
  student success;
• the role of accountability and accreditation when considering the methods
  to measure co-curricular learning;
• how co-curricular data align with university goals and priorities;
• the differences between direct and indirect measures of cocurricular
  learning; and
• the roles the institutional research office can play as a leader and
  collaborator in the measurement of co-curricular learning.
This volume is designed for institutional research professionals, student
affairs administrators, and all members of the university community
interested in measuring and communicating, via data, the holistic student
experience.
ISBN: 978-1-1192-2386-3

IR 163   **New Scholarship in Critical Quantitative Research—Part 2: New
Populations, Approaches, and Challenges**
Ryan S. Wells, Frances K. Stage
This volume of *New Directions for Institutional Research* is the second in a
two-part series differentiating approaches to quantitative research from more
traditional positivistic and postpositivistic approaches.
The term *quantitative criticalists* describes researchers who use quantitative
methods to represent educational processes and outcomes to reveal
inequities; question models, measures, and political processes; and resist
traditional quantitative research motivations that seek to solely confirm
theory and explain processes.
The first volume of this more recent series (#158) provided an expanded
conceptualization of critical quantitative inquiry and added an additional
task: to conduct culturally relevant research by studying institutions and
people in context. This volume concludes the series by:
• applying critical quantitative approaches to new populations of college
  students who are rarely addressed in institutional and higher education
  research, such as American Indian, Alaska Native, and students with
  disabilities,
• applying the principles of quantitative criticalism to advanced methods of
  statistical analysis, and
• discussing the variety of challenges to overcome and presenting a future
  research agenda using these methods.
This work is of interest to institutional and higher education researchers who
want to expand and critique new ways of thinking about the broad array of

populations participating in and served by higher education, while keeping in mind the goals of revealing inequity, challenging marginalization, and helping all students to succeed.
ISBN: 978-1-1191-0188-8

IR 162 **Assessing Civic Engagement**
Dawn Geronimo Terkla, Lisa S. O'Leary
How does one assess community service, civic engagement, and the impact of service learning on a college campus? How does one measure this somewhat elusive phenomenon that is defined in many different ways? This can be discussed within the framework of the seemingly reciprocal relationship between campus environment and civic engagement outcomes. This volume reviews contemporary research, measurement instruments, and practices in the assessment of civic engagement in higher education, including:
- meta-analyses of students, faculty, institutions, and higher education systems at-large,
- targeted case studies of campus-specific practices at individual institutions,
- efficient and effective ways to gauge the influence of civic engagement on higher education policy, practices, and outcomes, and
- quantitative and qualitative approaches to measuring the effort, importance of, and impact of students' and institutions' involvement in community service, community engagement, civic engagement, and service learning on a college campus.

The research ranges between decisions made either as part of institutional agendas, curricular enhancements, or student life initiatives and student and professor involvement in civic engagement activities and supportive attitudes. This will be of interest to faculty, administrators, student affairs professionals, and other staff involved with curricular and cocurricular programs.
ISBN: 978-1-1190-6505-0

IR 161 **Methodological Advances and Issues in Studying College Impact**
Nicholas A. Bowman, Serge Herzog
Many constituents within and outside of higher education have demanded strong evidence about which curricular and cocurricular practices promote student learning and persistence. However, most research and assessment on college student outcomes currently offers limited insight into causal effects. This volume of *New Directions for Institutional Research* provides resources and information to improve the quality of work examining the impact of college on students. The first section discusses statistical analyses that offer more accurate estimates of the causal effect of a particular student experience, such as receiving a need-based scholarship or using academic support services. These chapters provide an overview of the analytical framework and real-world examples to illustrate implementation for institutional researchers. The second section includes original research to enhance the value of student surveys, including:
- aspects of questionnaire design and techniques to cope with item nonresponse,
- variation in respondent effort,
- interpretation of student self-reported gains, and
- practical insights to improve survey-based research.

The findings should be of interest to institutional research practitioners, higher education scholars, and those seeking to understand effects of the college experience.
ISBN: 978-1-1190-4561-8

NEW DIRECTIONS FOR INSTITUTIONAL RESEARCH

ORDER FORM SUBSCRIPTION AND SINGLE ISSUES

DISCOUNTED BACK ISSUES:

Use this form to receive 20% off all back issues of *New Directions for Institutional Research*.
All single issues priced at **$23.20** (normally $29.00)

TITLE	ISSUE NO.	ISBN

Call 1-800-835-6770 or see mailing instructions below. When calling, mention the promotional code JBNND to receive your discount. For a complete list of issues, please visit www.wiley.com/WileyCDA/WileyTitle/productCd-IR.html

SUBSCRIPTIONS: (1 YEAR, 4 ISSUES)

☐ New Order ☐ Renewal

U.S.	☐ Individual: $89	☐ Institutional: $362
CANADA/MEXICO	☐ Individual: $89	☐ Institutional: $404
ALL OTHERS	☐ Individual: $113	☐ Institutional: $440

Call 1-800-835-6770 or see mailing and pricing instructions below.
Online subscriptions are available at www.onlinelibrary.wiley.com

ORDER TOTALS:

Issue / Subscription Amount: $ _____

Shipping Amount: $ _____
(for single issues only – subscription prices include shipping)

Total Amount: $ _____

SHIPPING CHARGES:
First Item $6.00
Each Add'l Item $2.00

(No sales tax for U.S. subscriptions. Canadian residents, add GST for subscription orders. Individual rate subscriptions must be paid by personal check or credit card. Individual rate subscriptions may not be resold as library copies.)

BILLING & SHIPPING INFORMATION:

☐ **PAYMENT ENCLOSED:** *(U.S. check or money order only. All payments must be in U.S. dollars.)*

☐ **CREDIT CARD:** ☐ VISA ☐ MC ☐ AMEX

Card number _____ Exp. Date _____

Card Holder Name _____ Card Issue # _____

Signature _____ Day Phone _____

☐ **BILL ME:** *(U.S. institutional orders only. Purchase order required.)*

Purchase order # _____
Federal Tax ID 13559302 • GST 89102-8052

Name _____

Address _____

Phone _____ E-mail _____

Copy or detach page and send to: **John Wiley & Sons, Inc. / Jossey Bass**
PO Box 55381
Boston, MA 02205-9850

PROMO JBNND

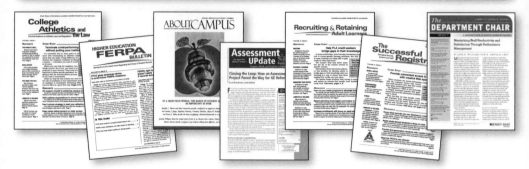